I0465802

THIS COLORING BOOK BELONGS TO:

....

DATE:

....

Some graphic elements in this book have been created by Drawnhy97, Doodle_flower, Onfocus, GarryKillian, Rawpixel.com, Pikisuperstar at Freepik.com

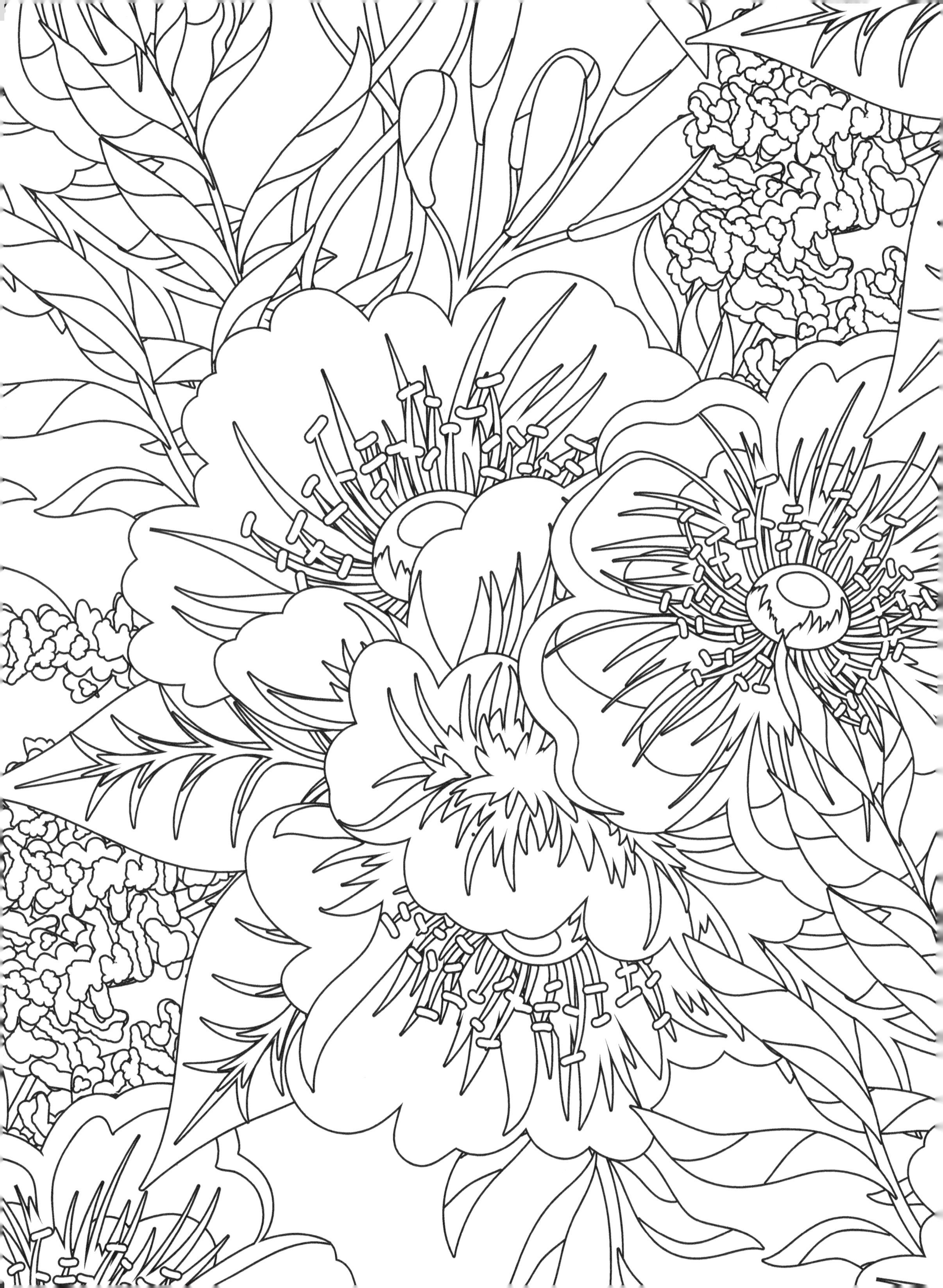

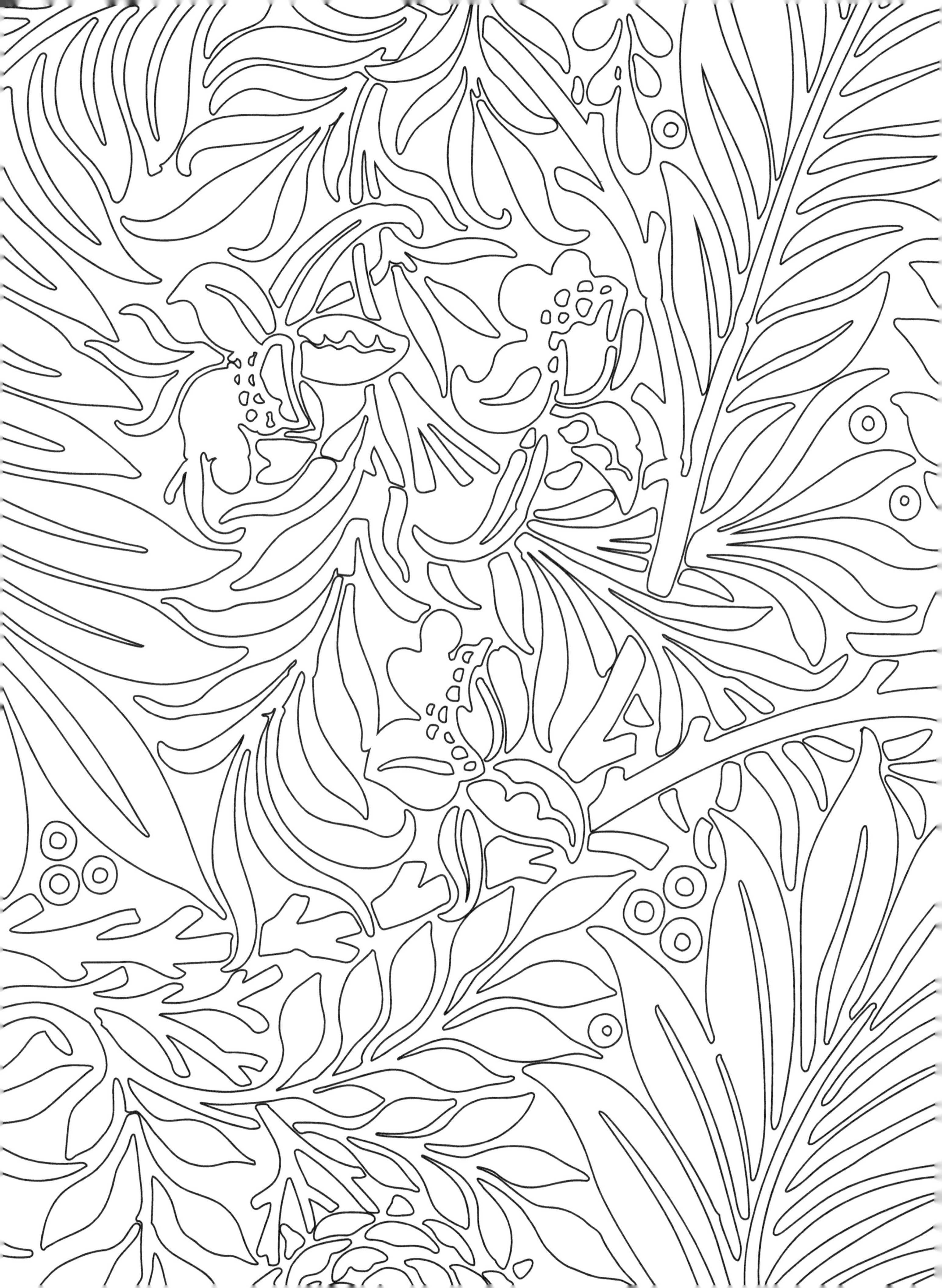

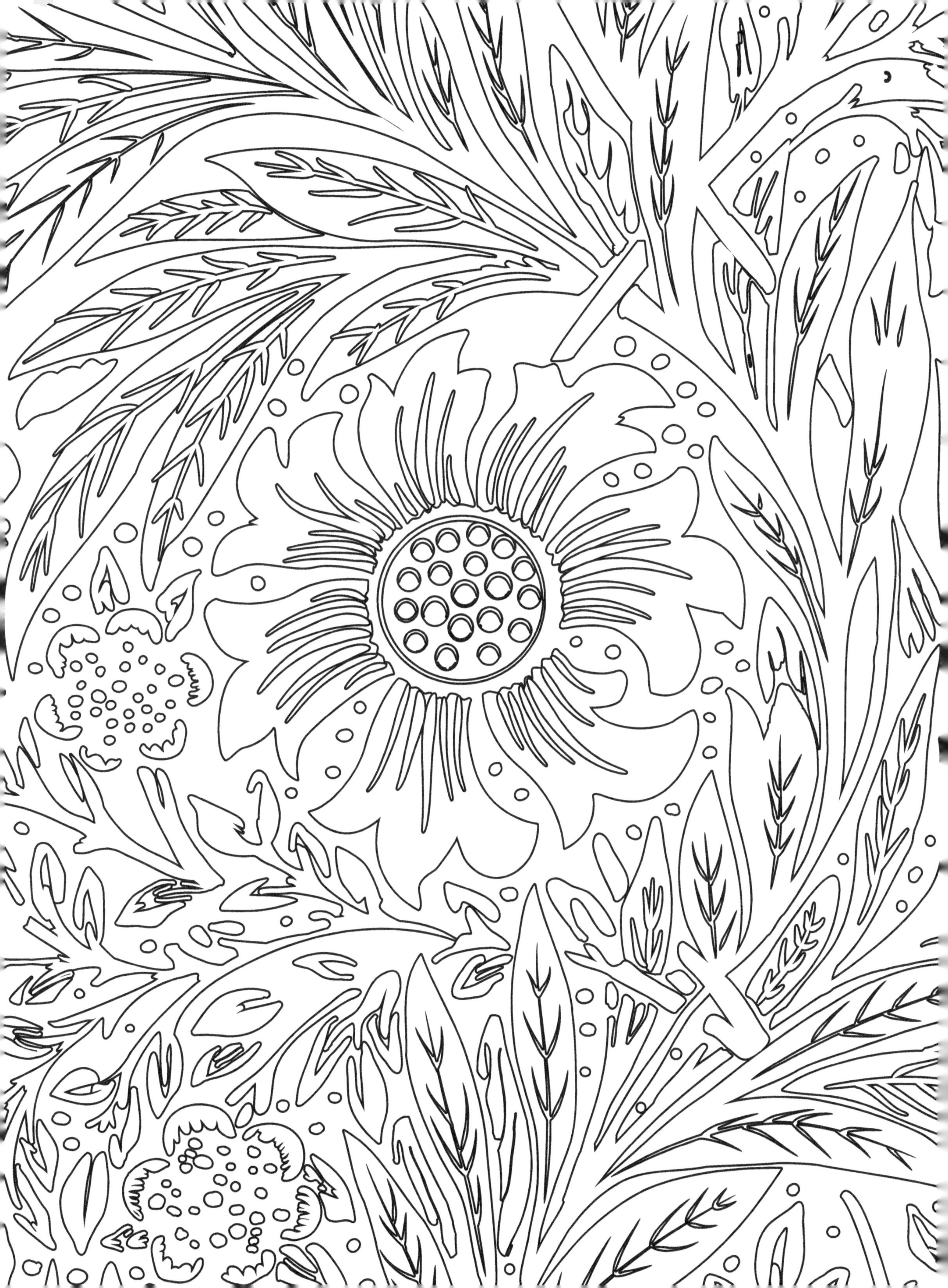

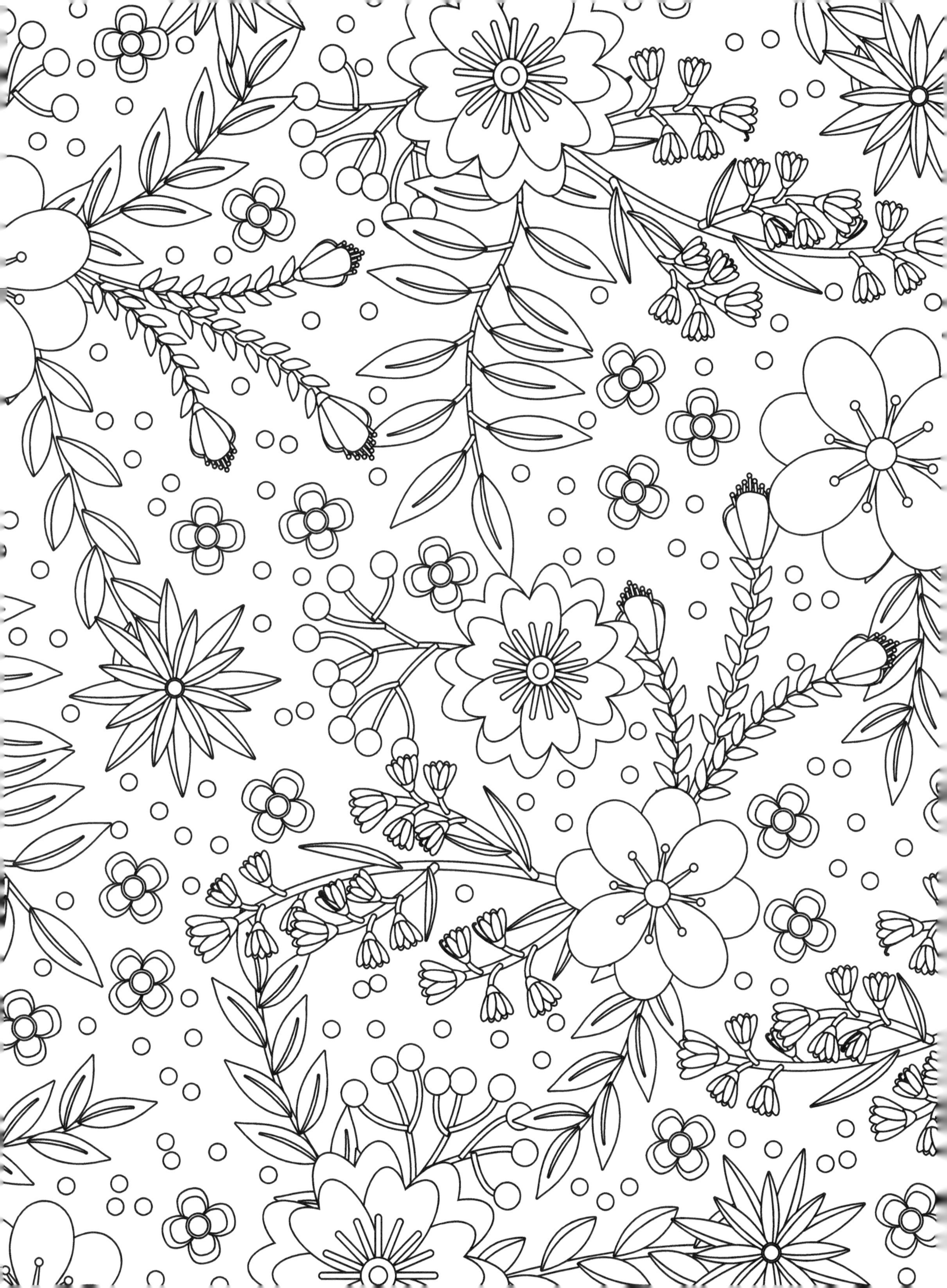

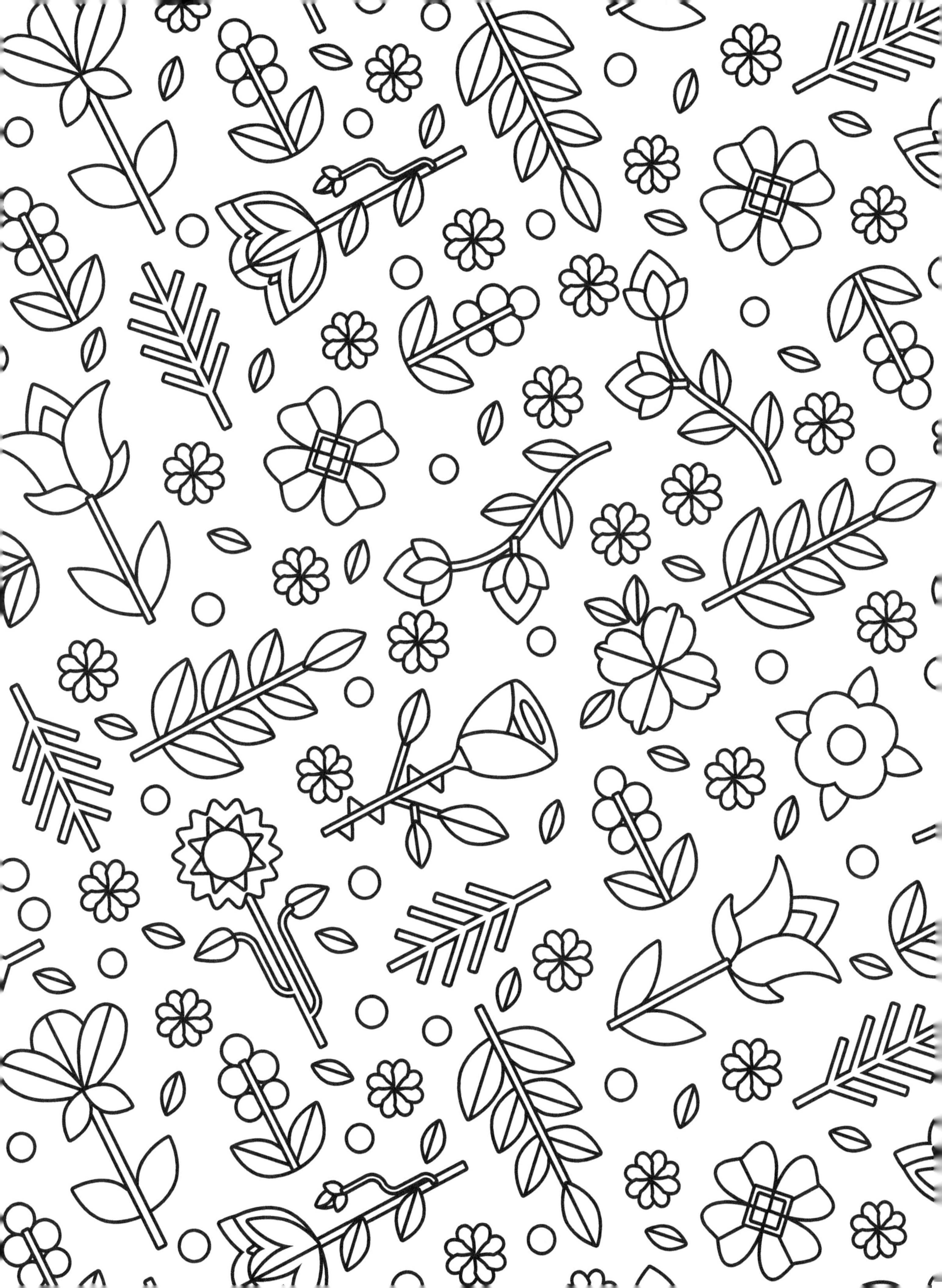

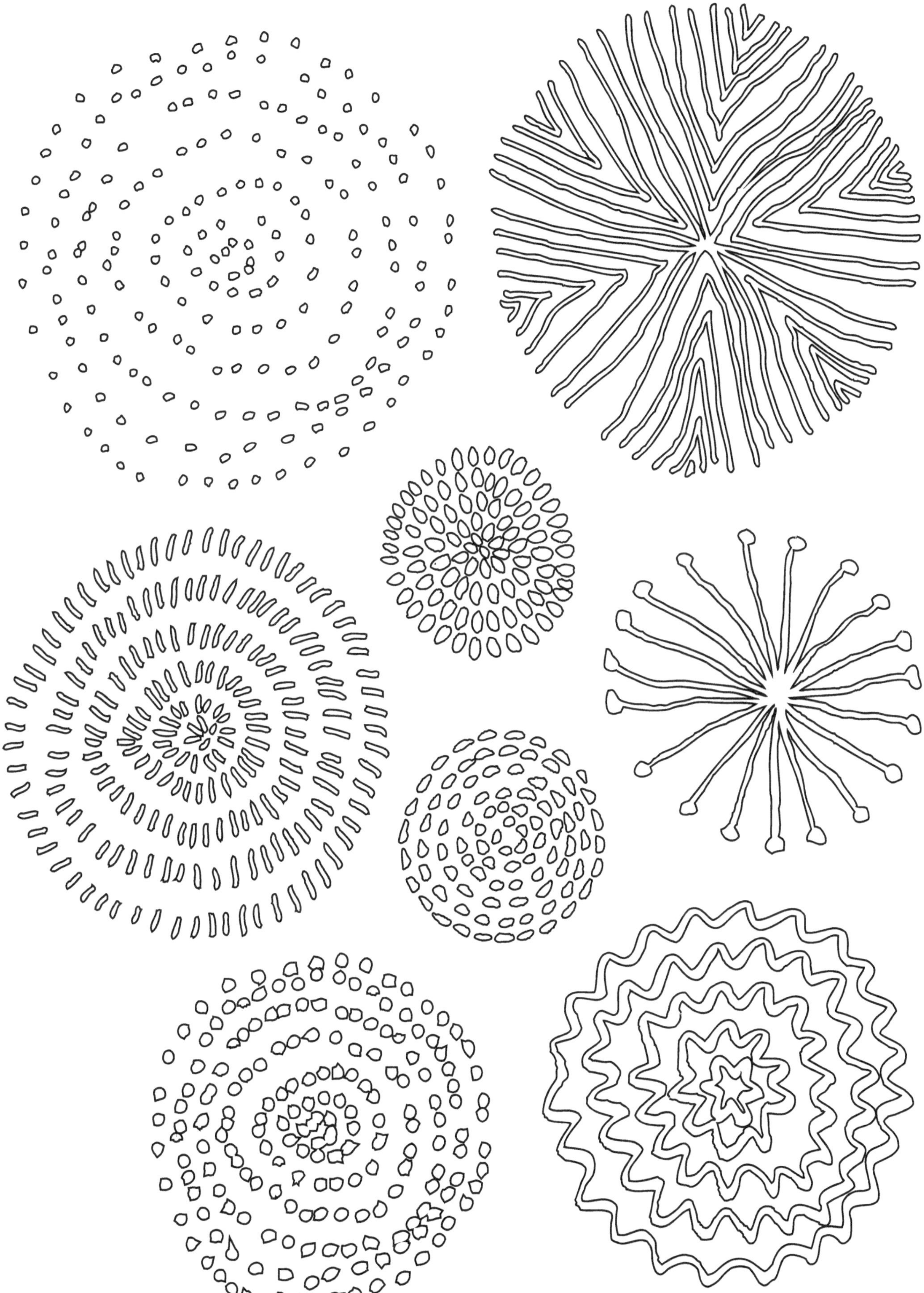

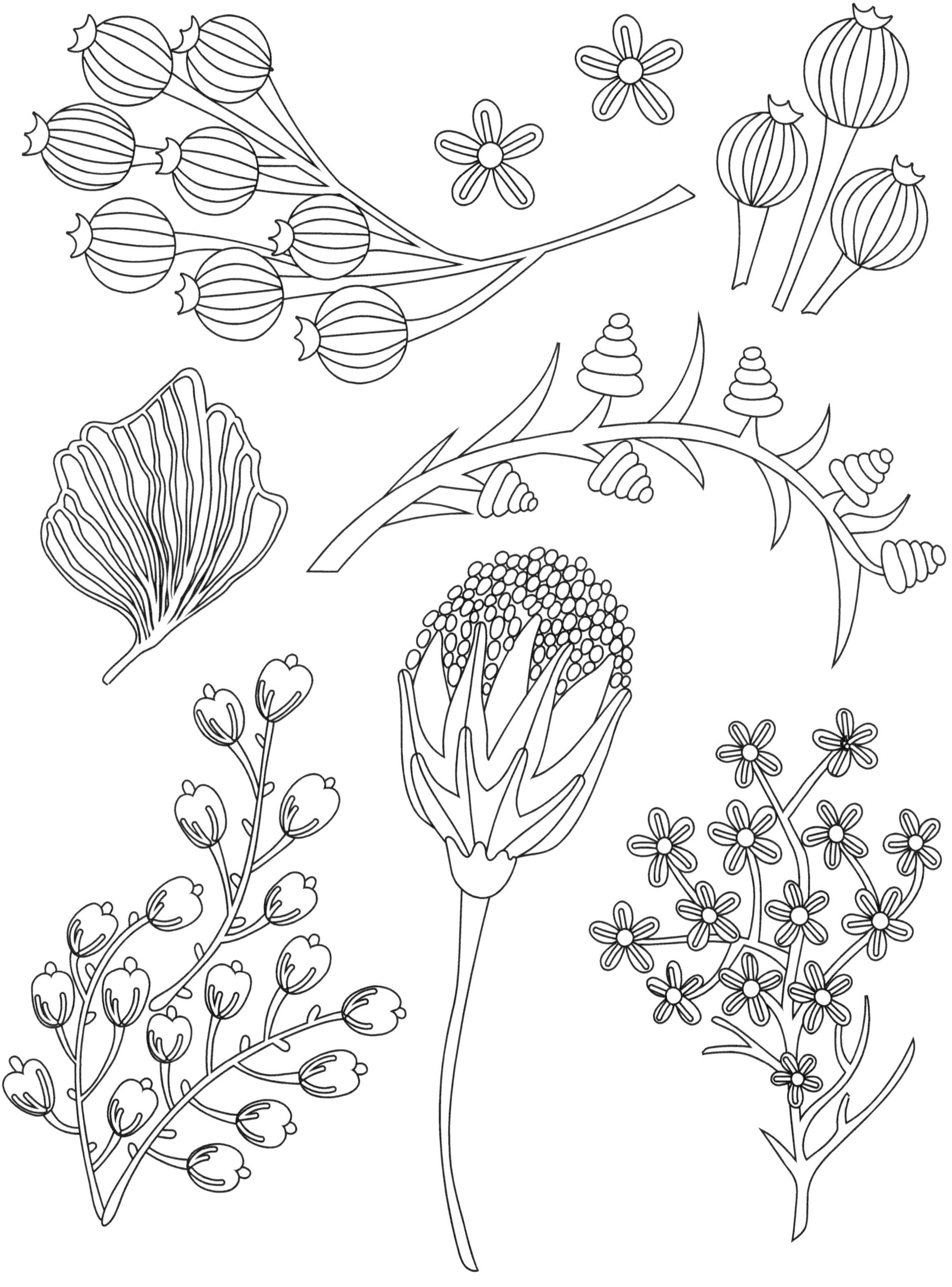

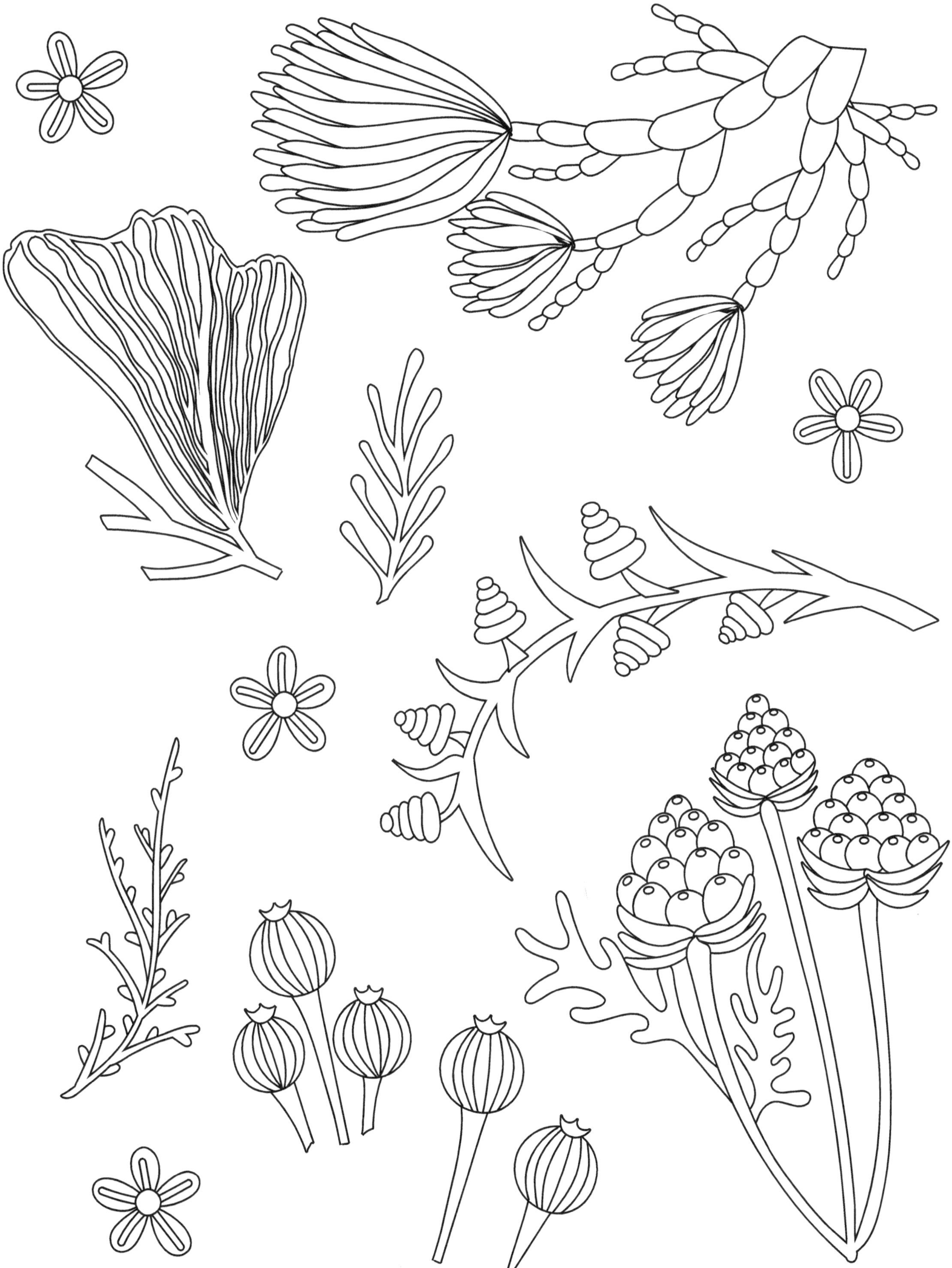

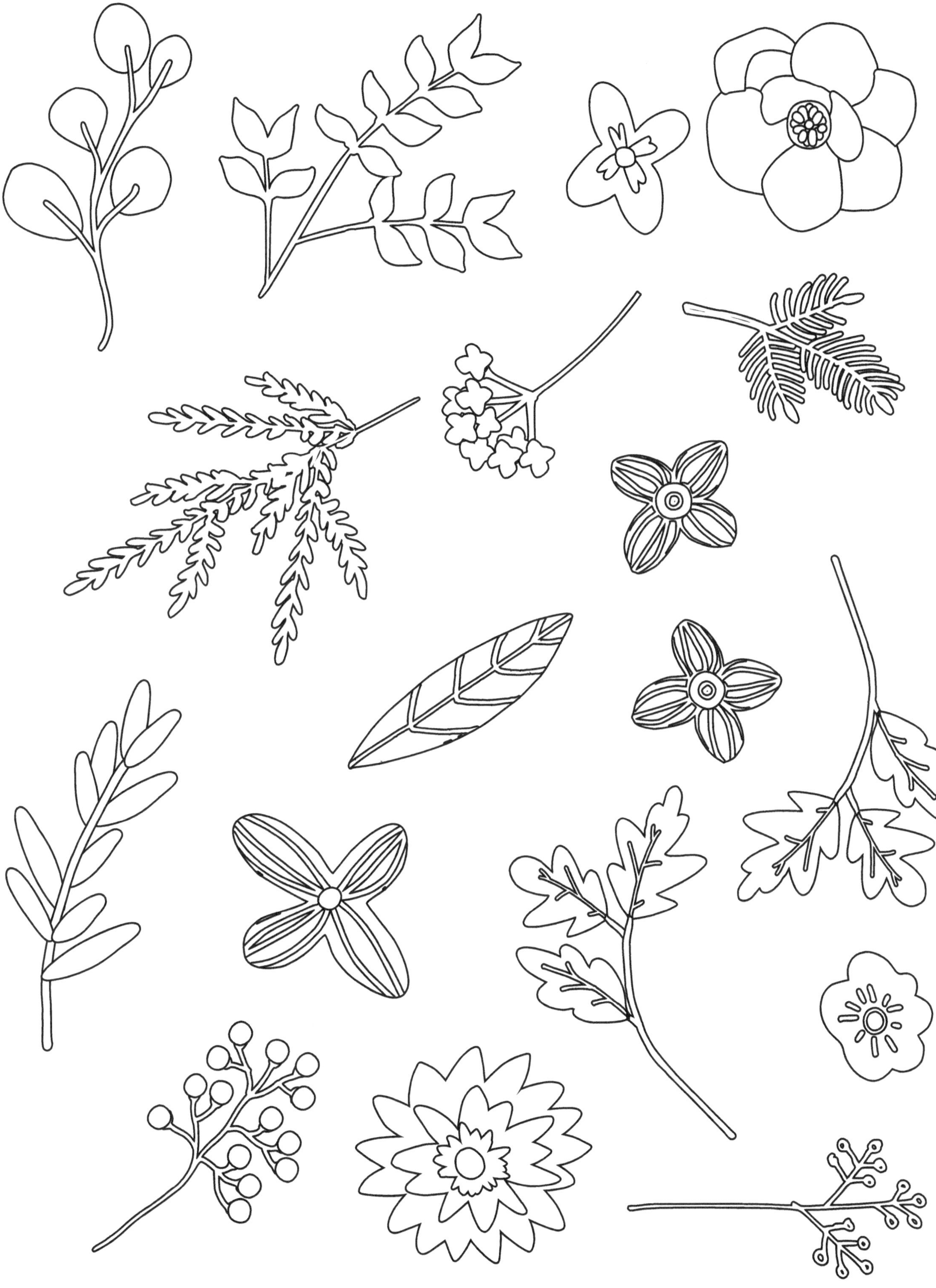

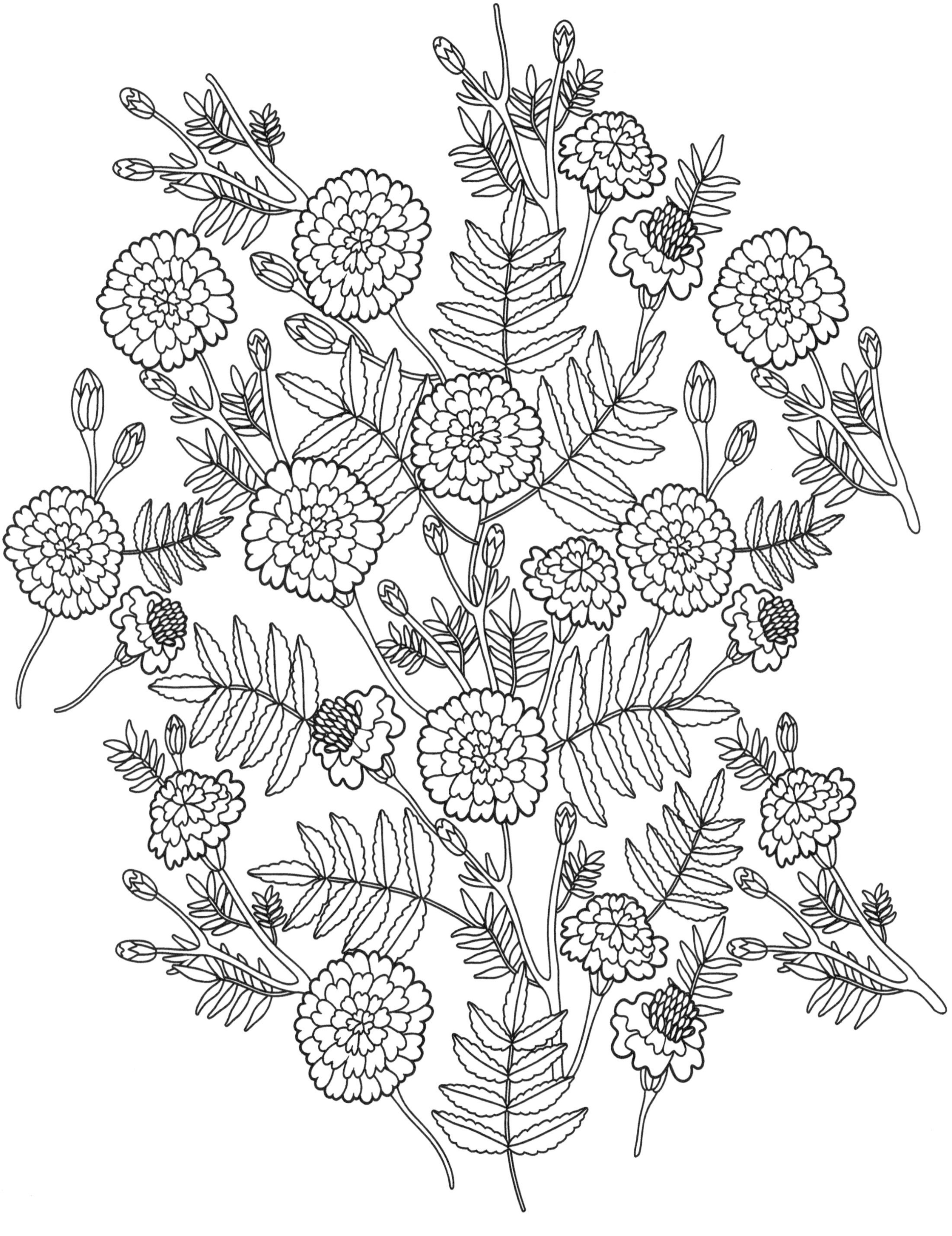

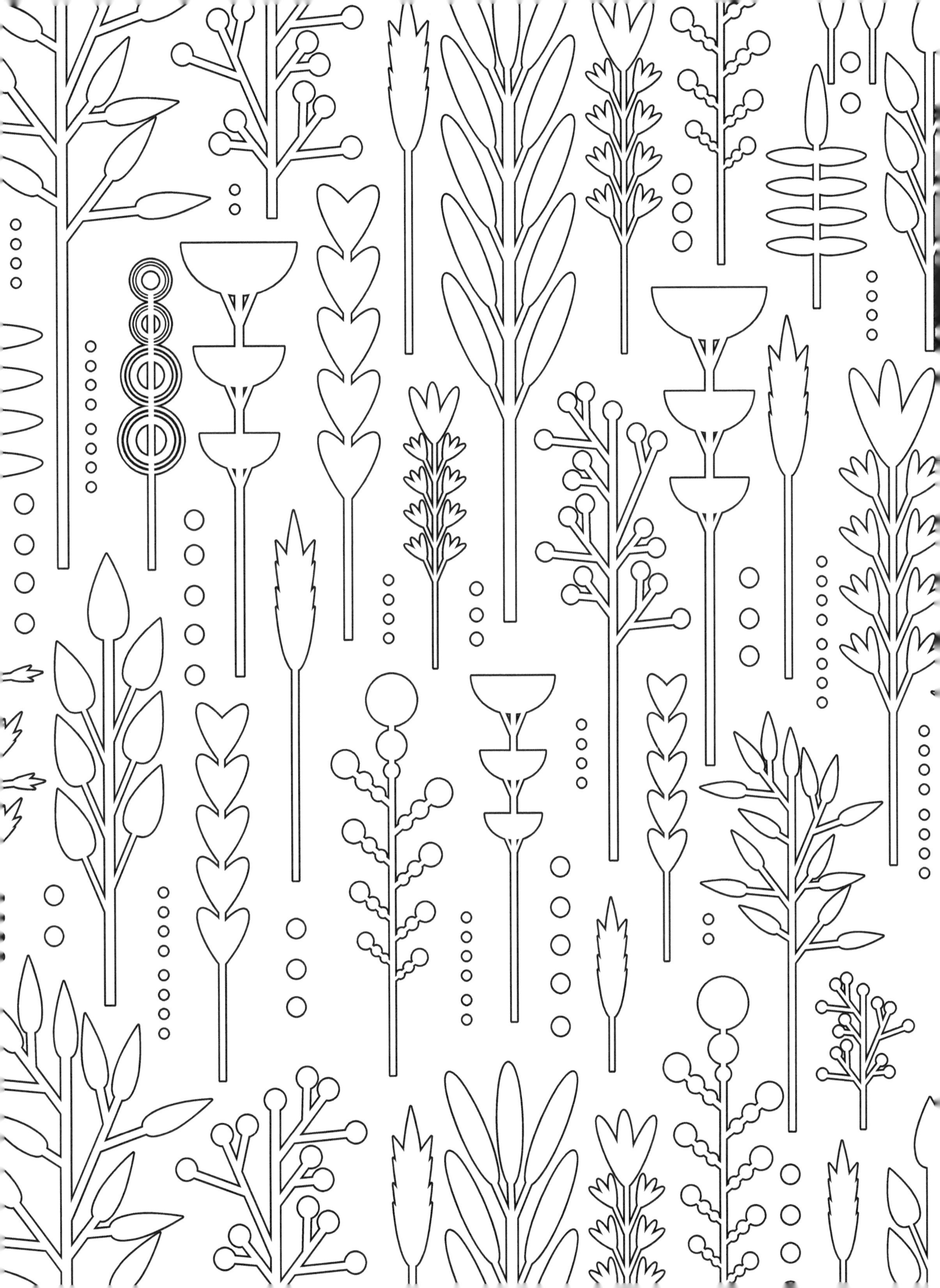

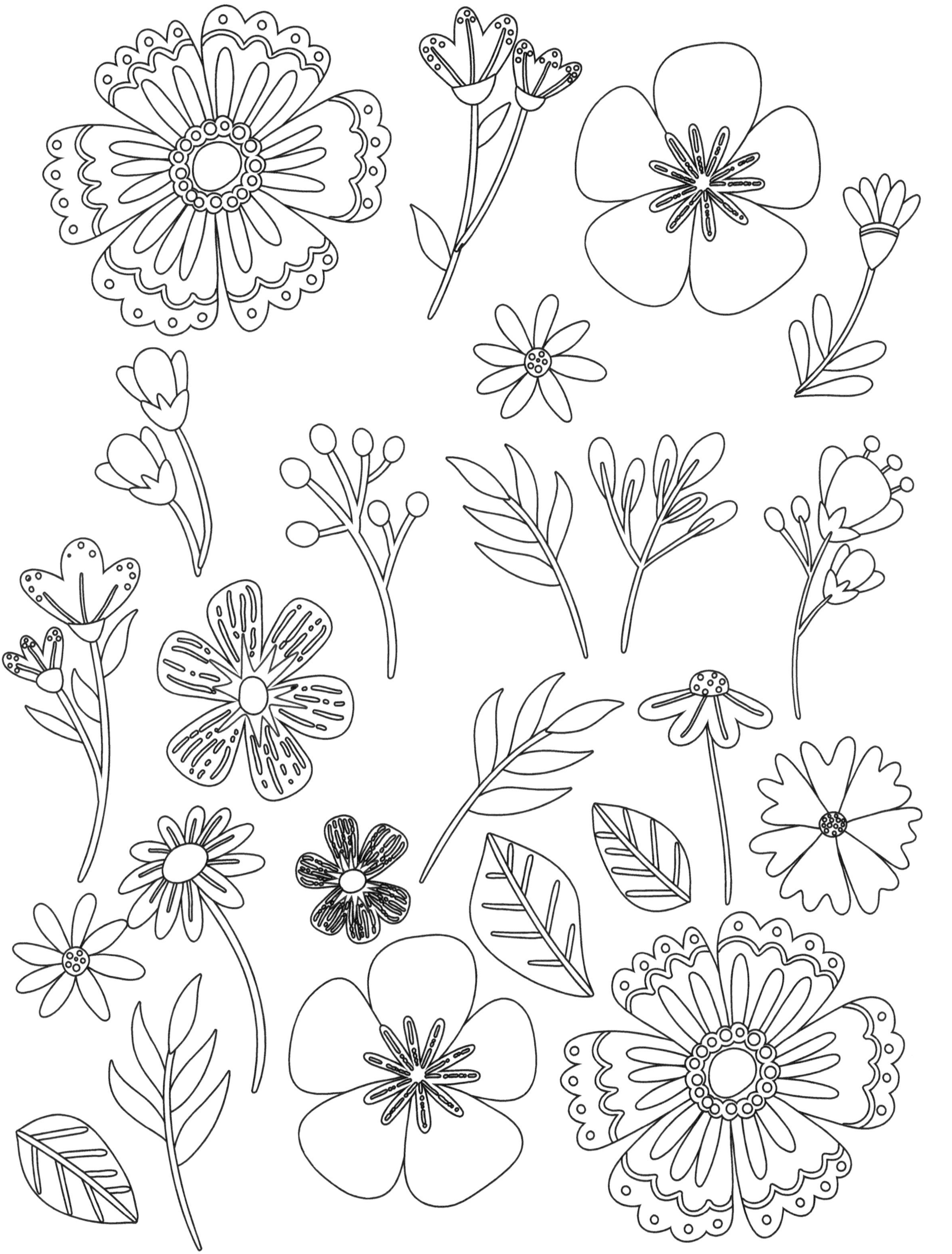

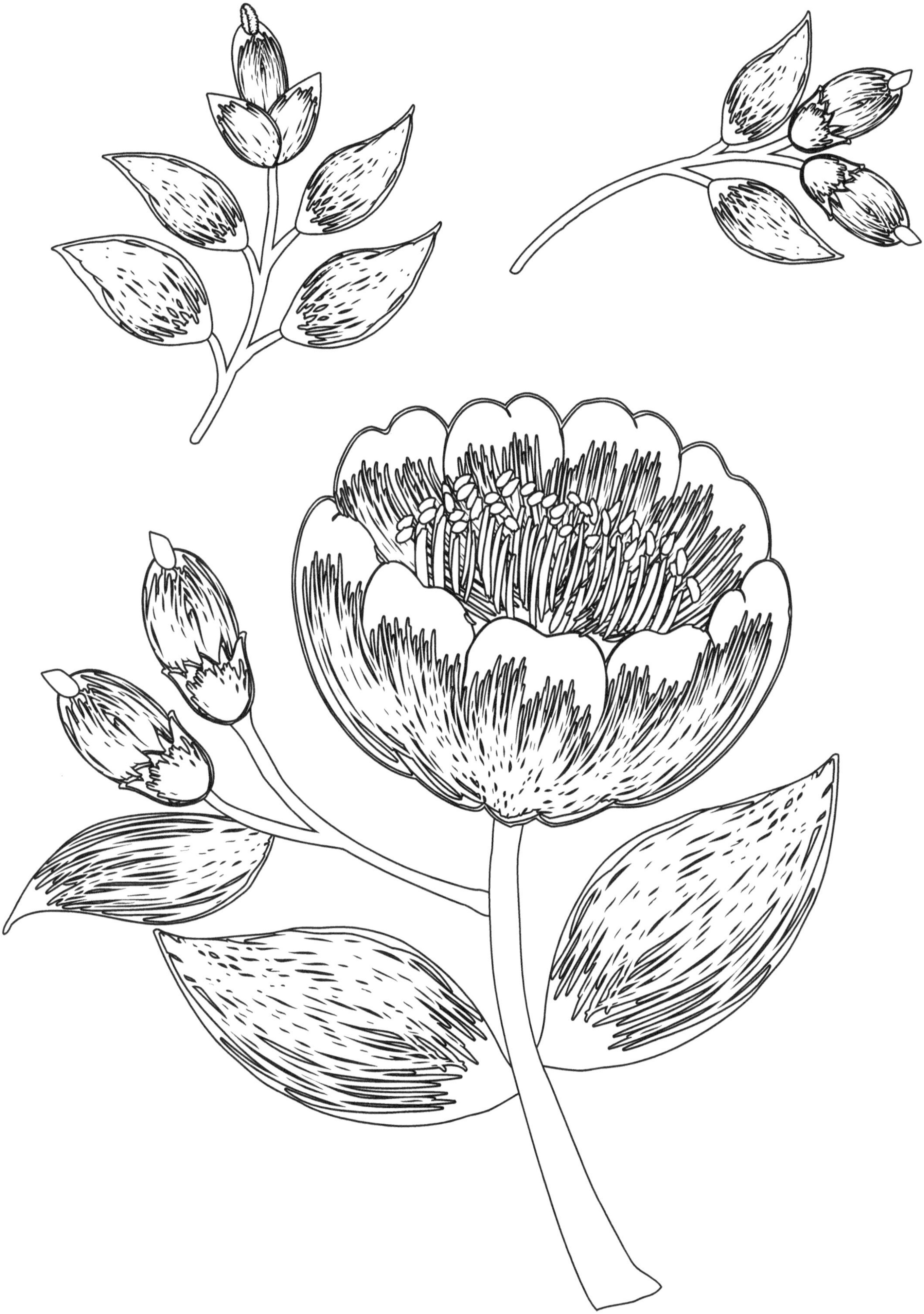

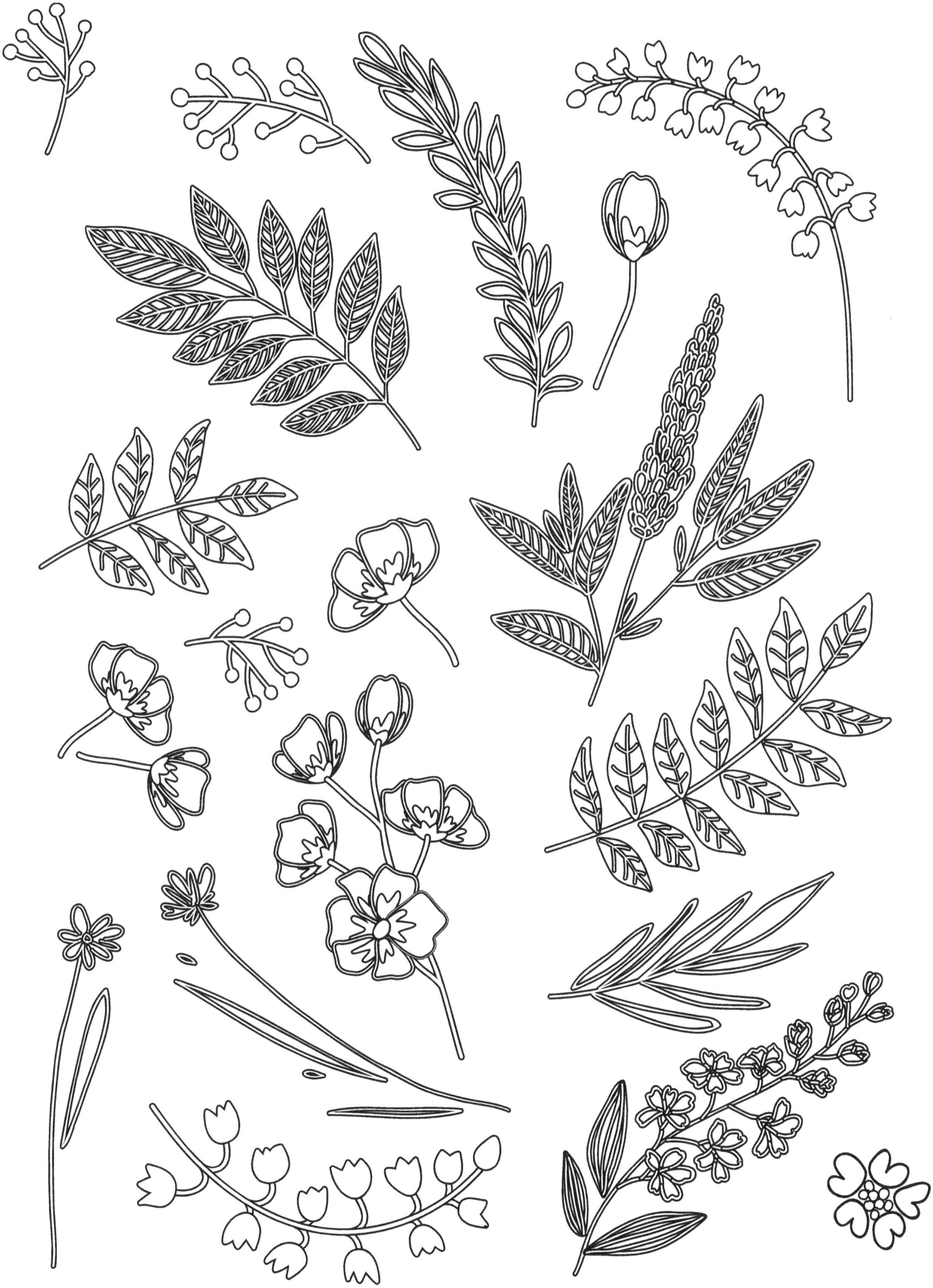

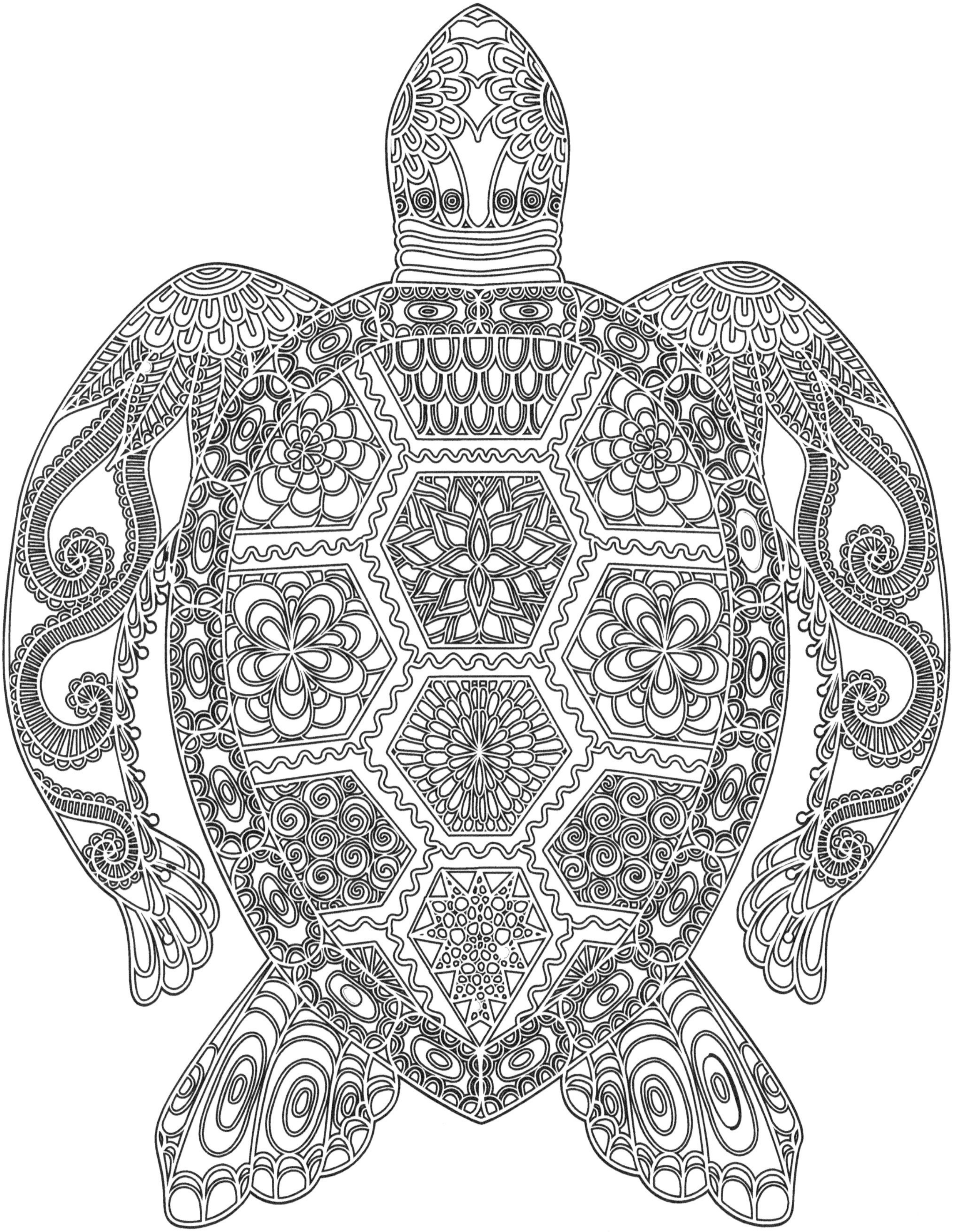

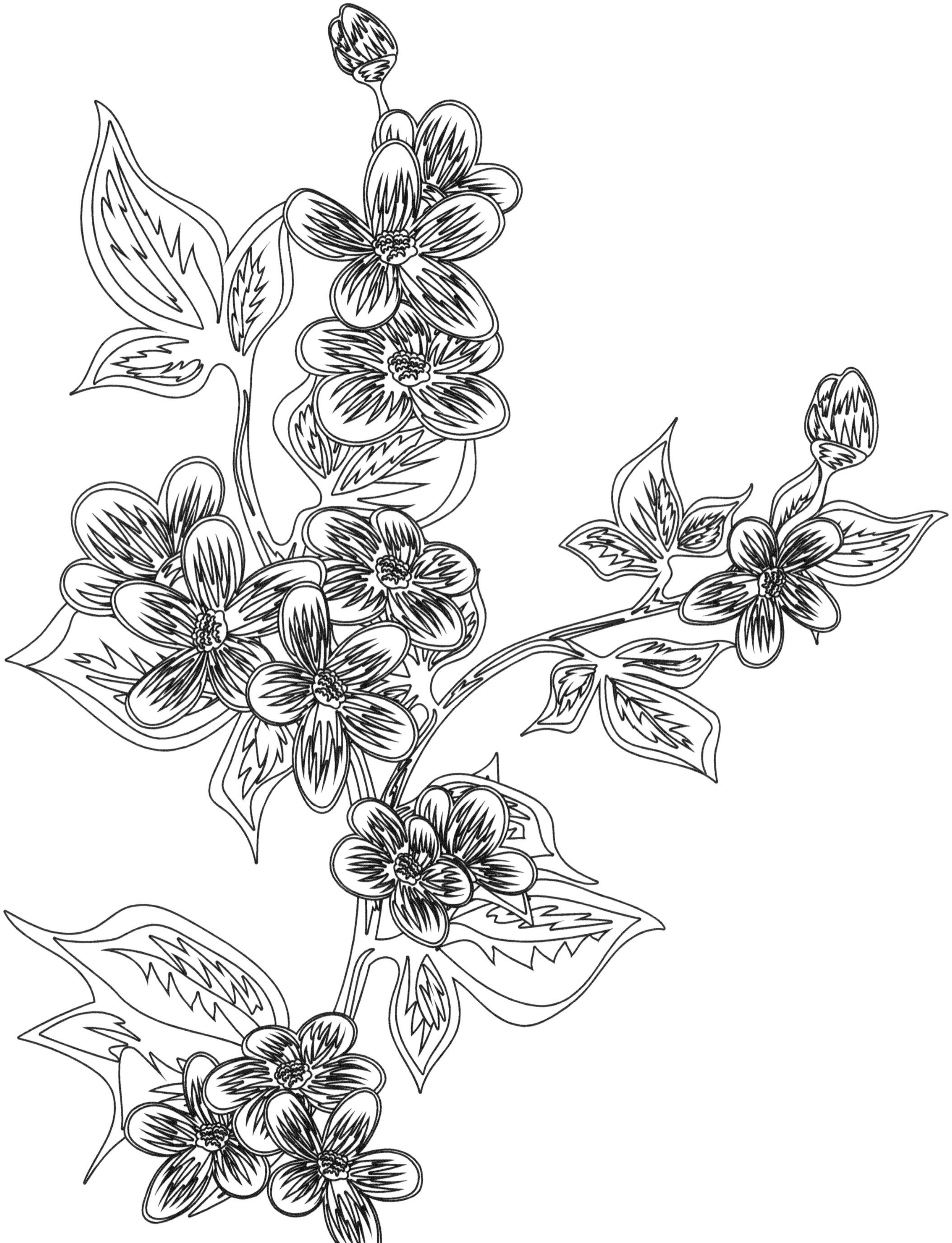

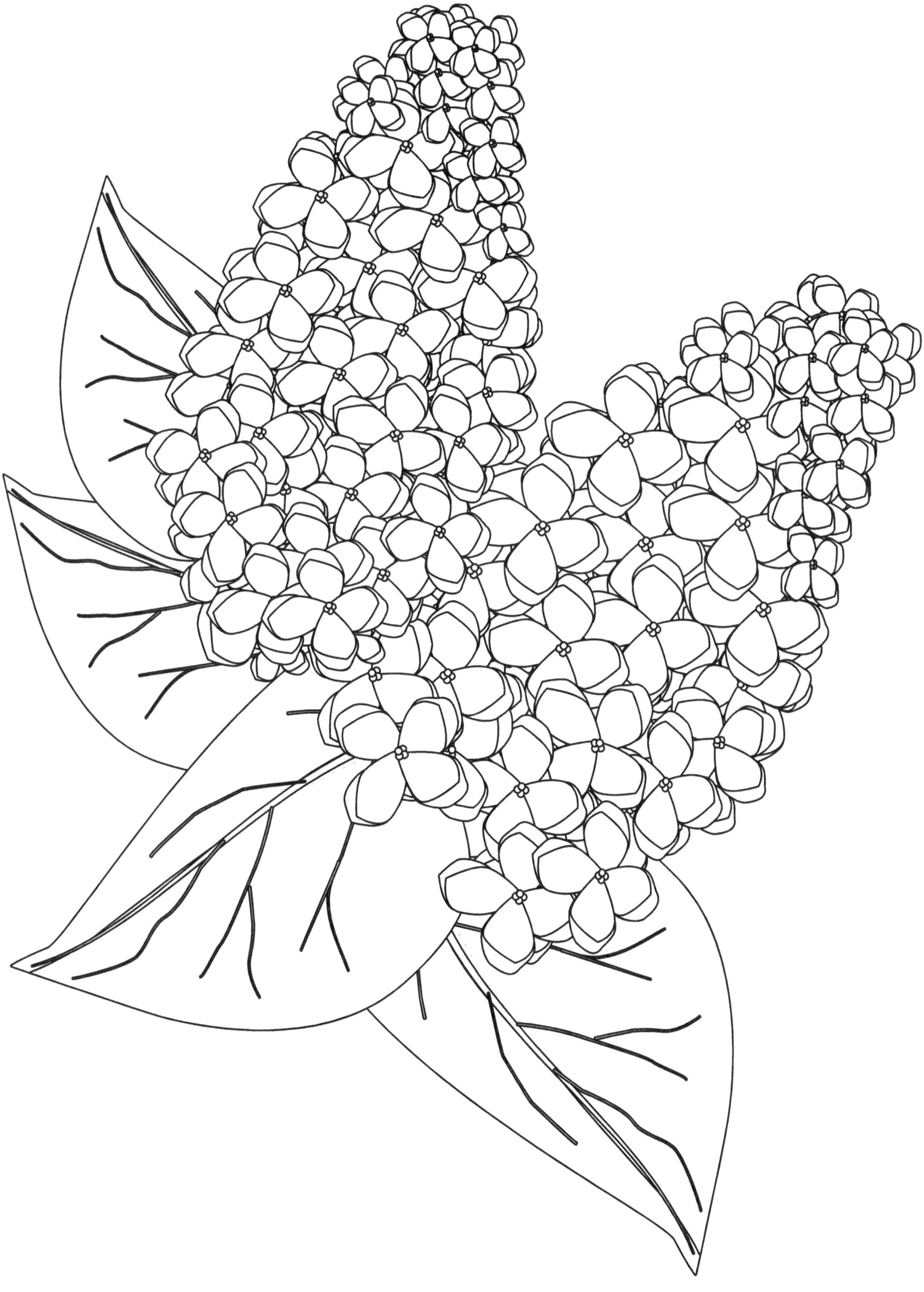

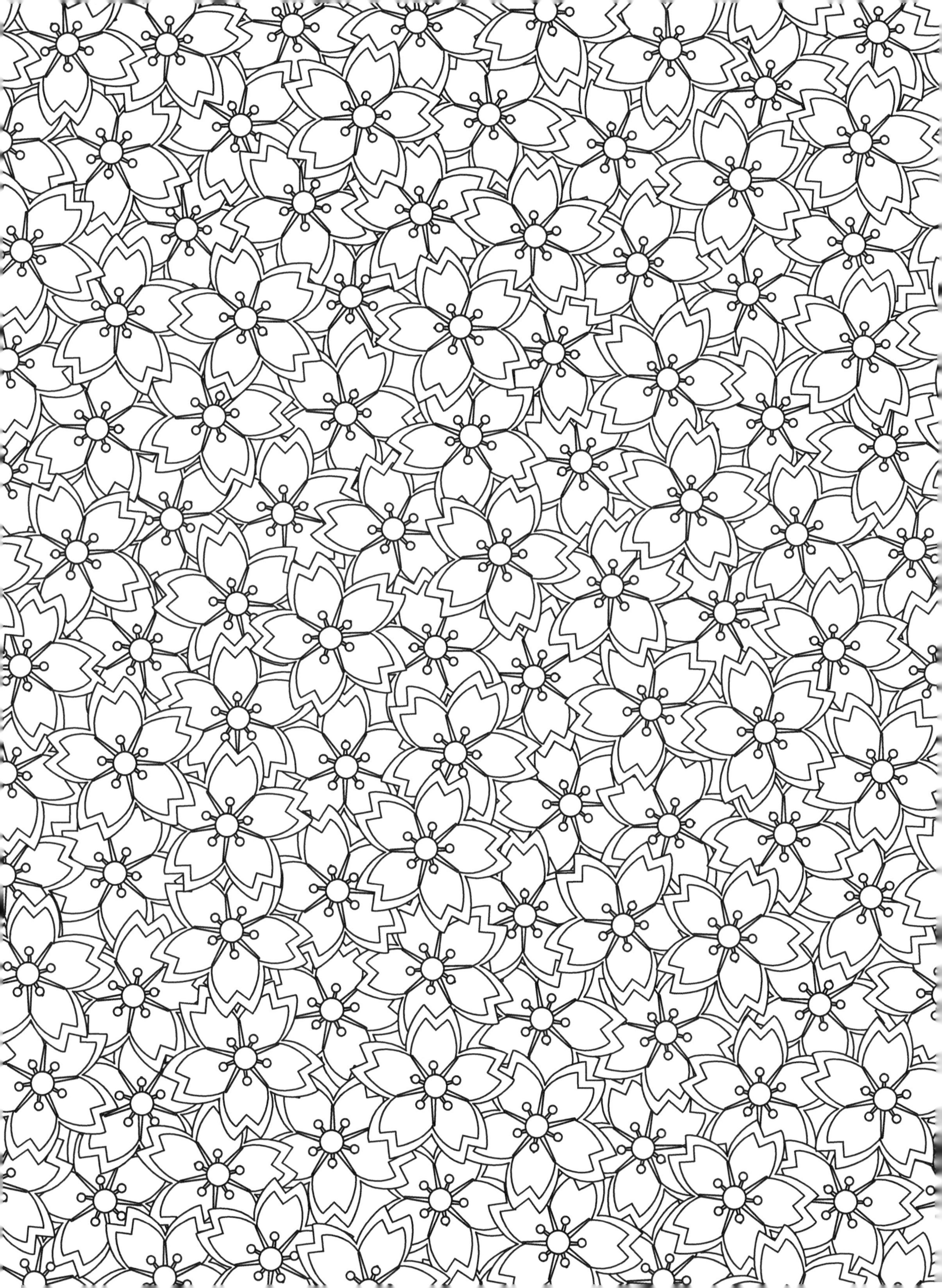

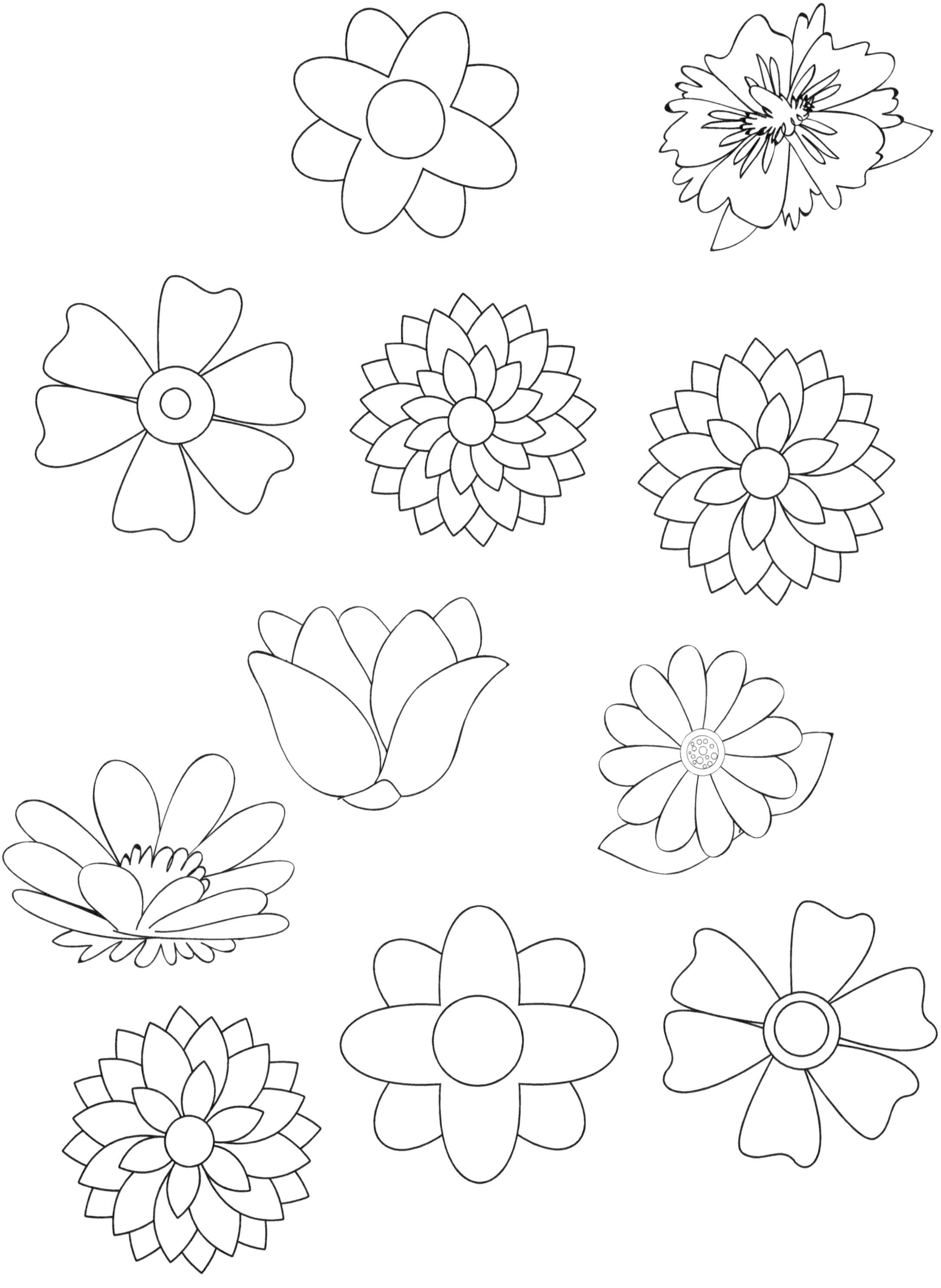

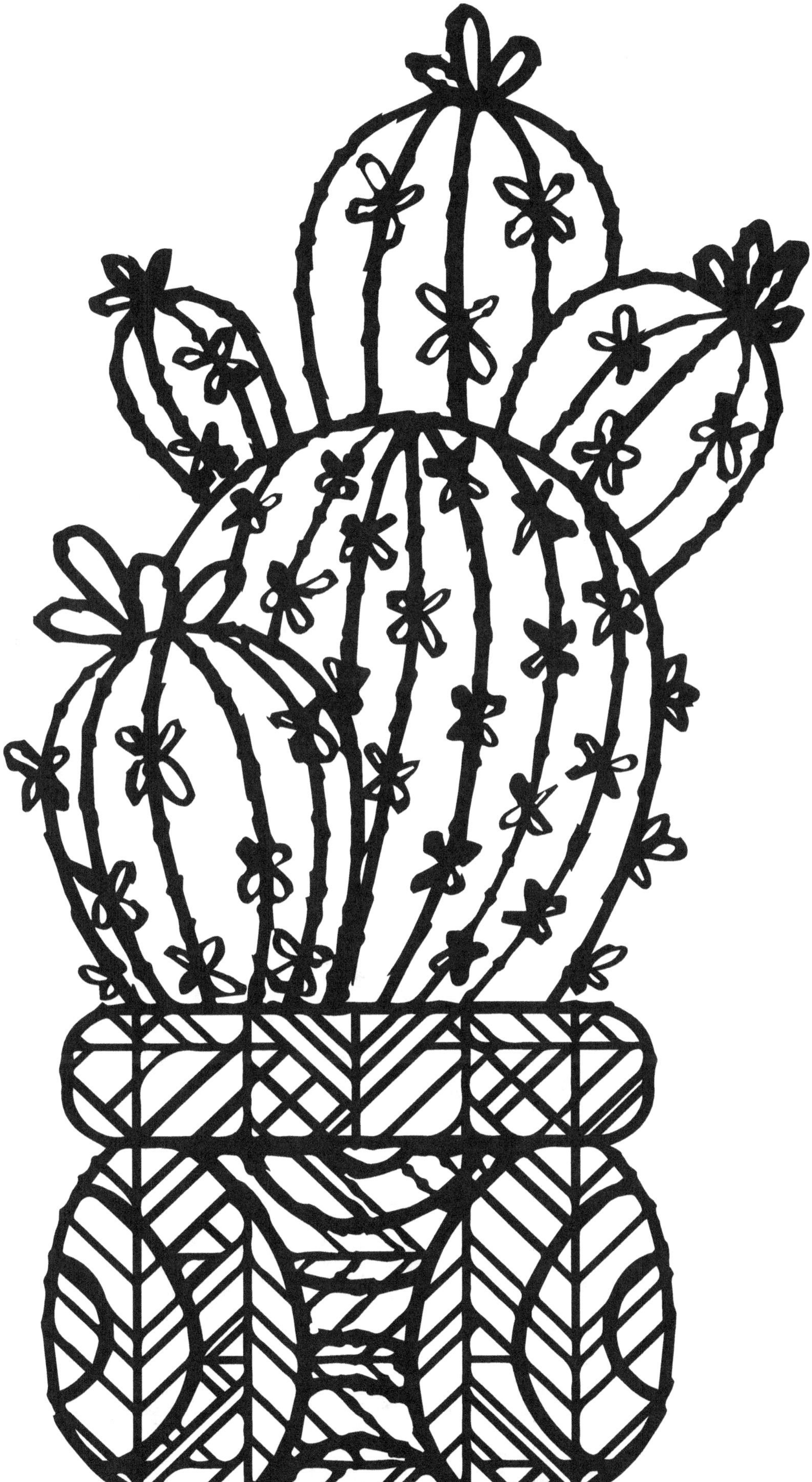

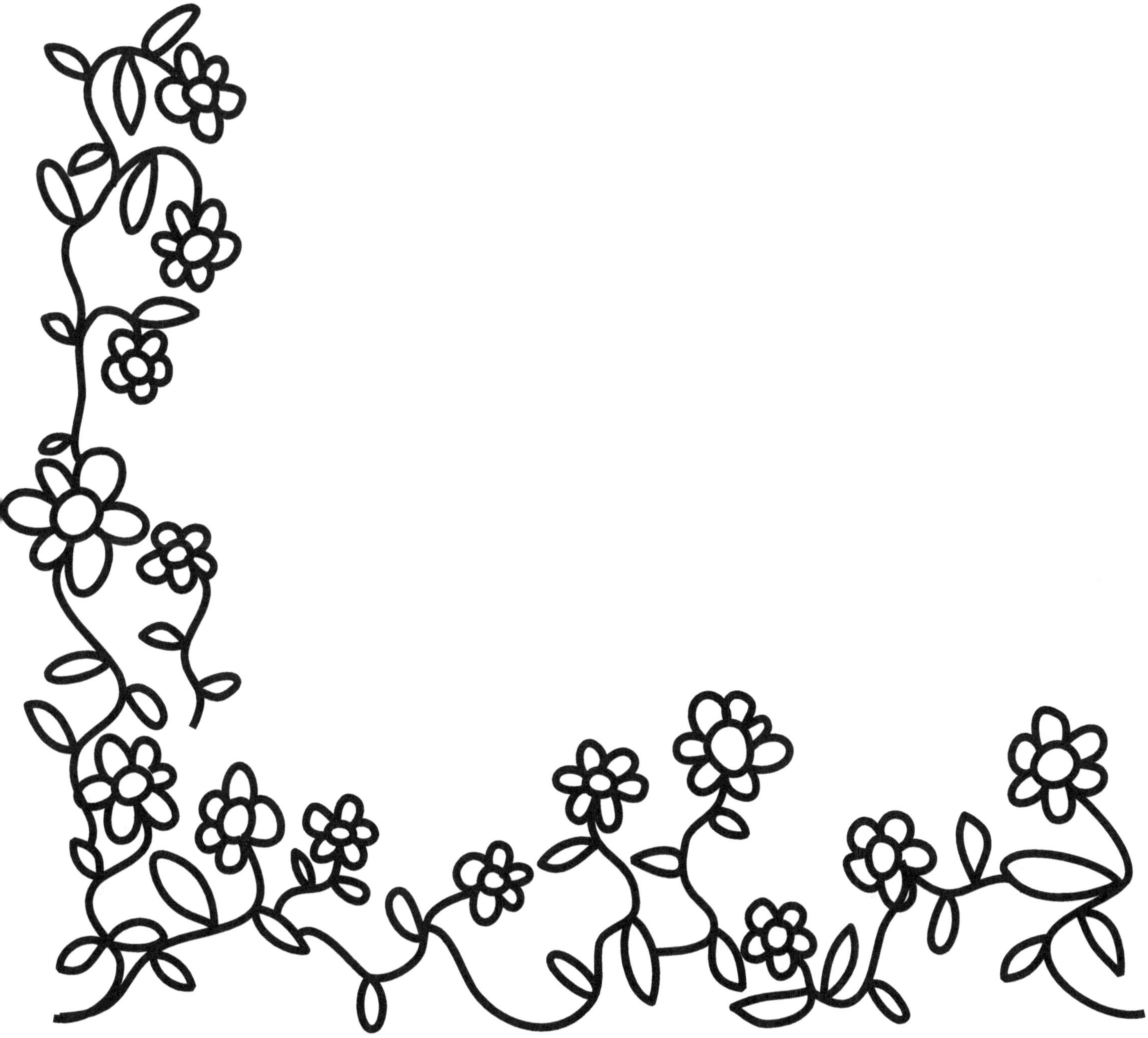

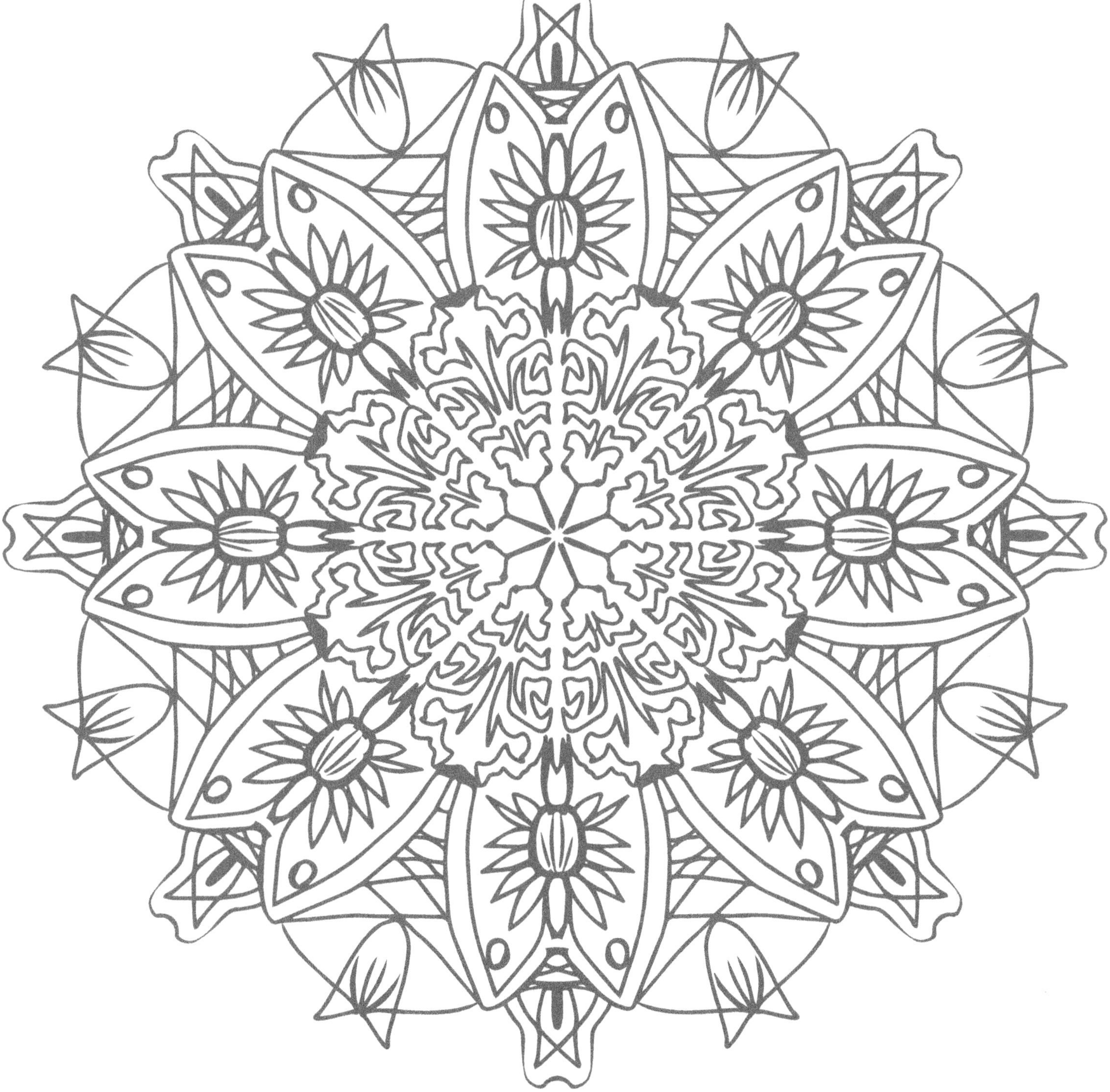

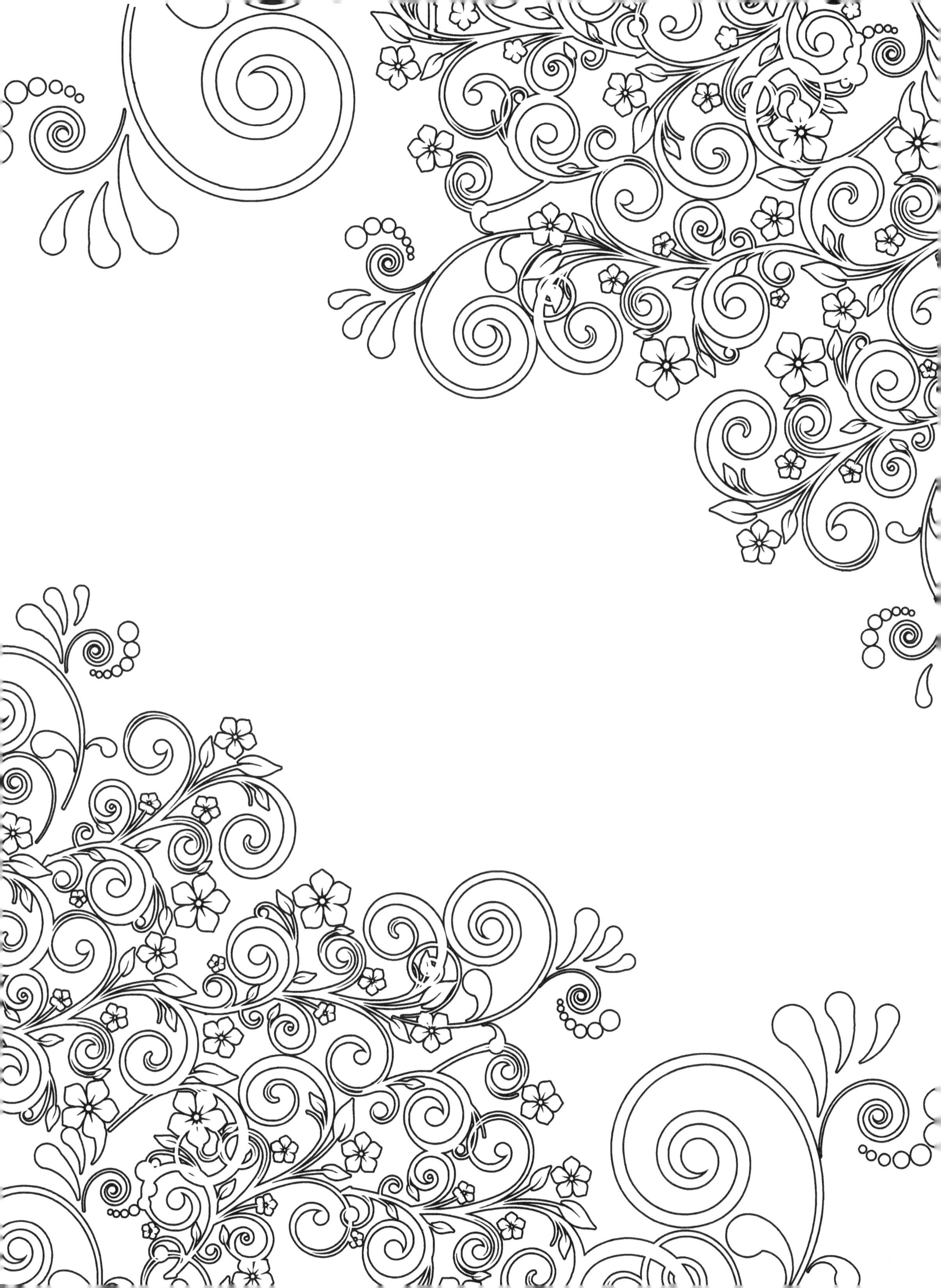

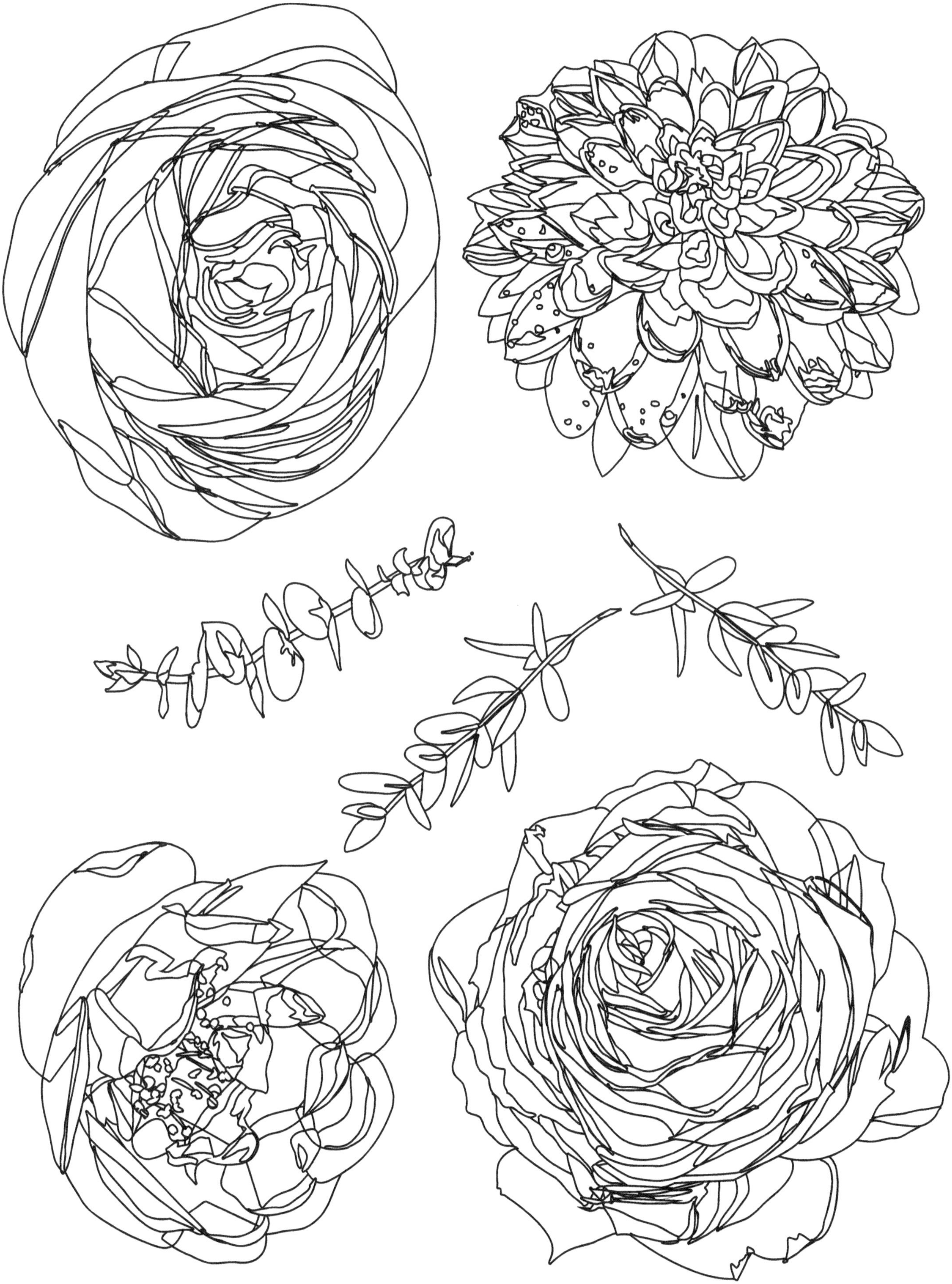

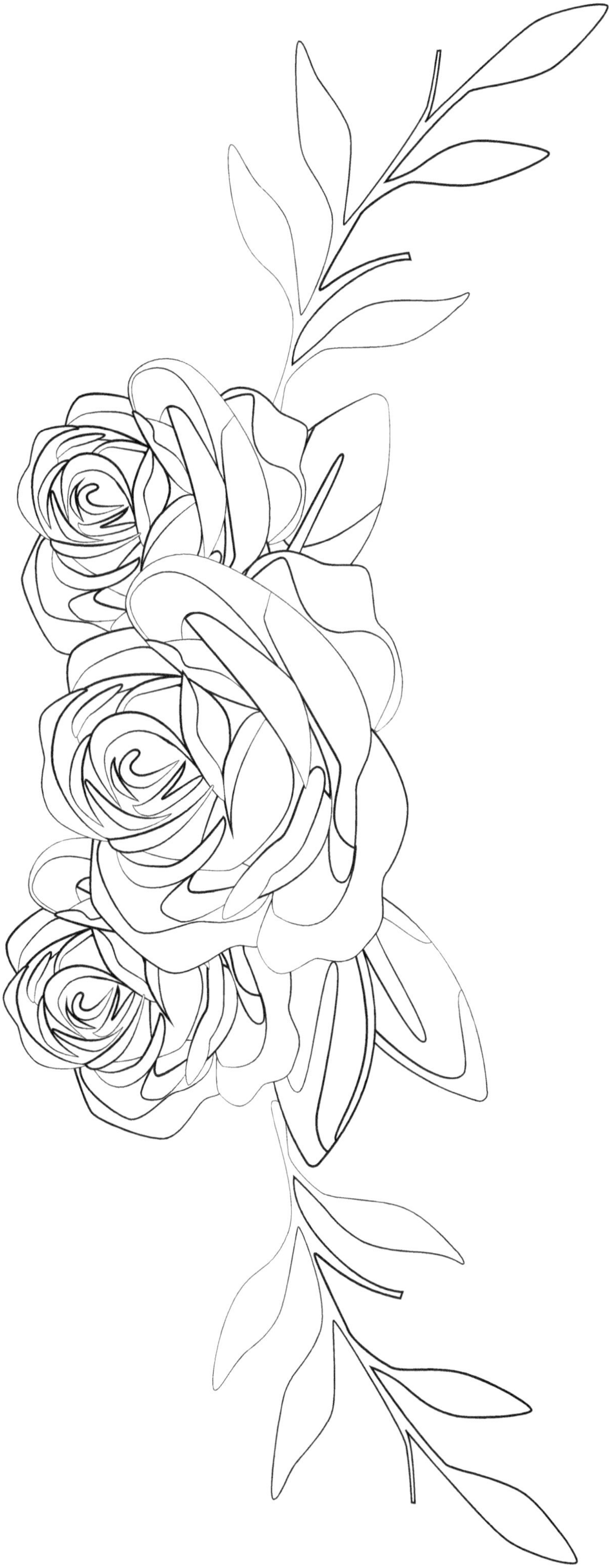

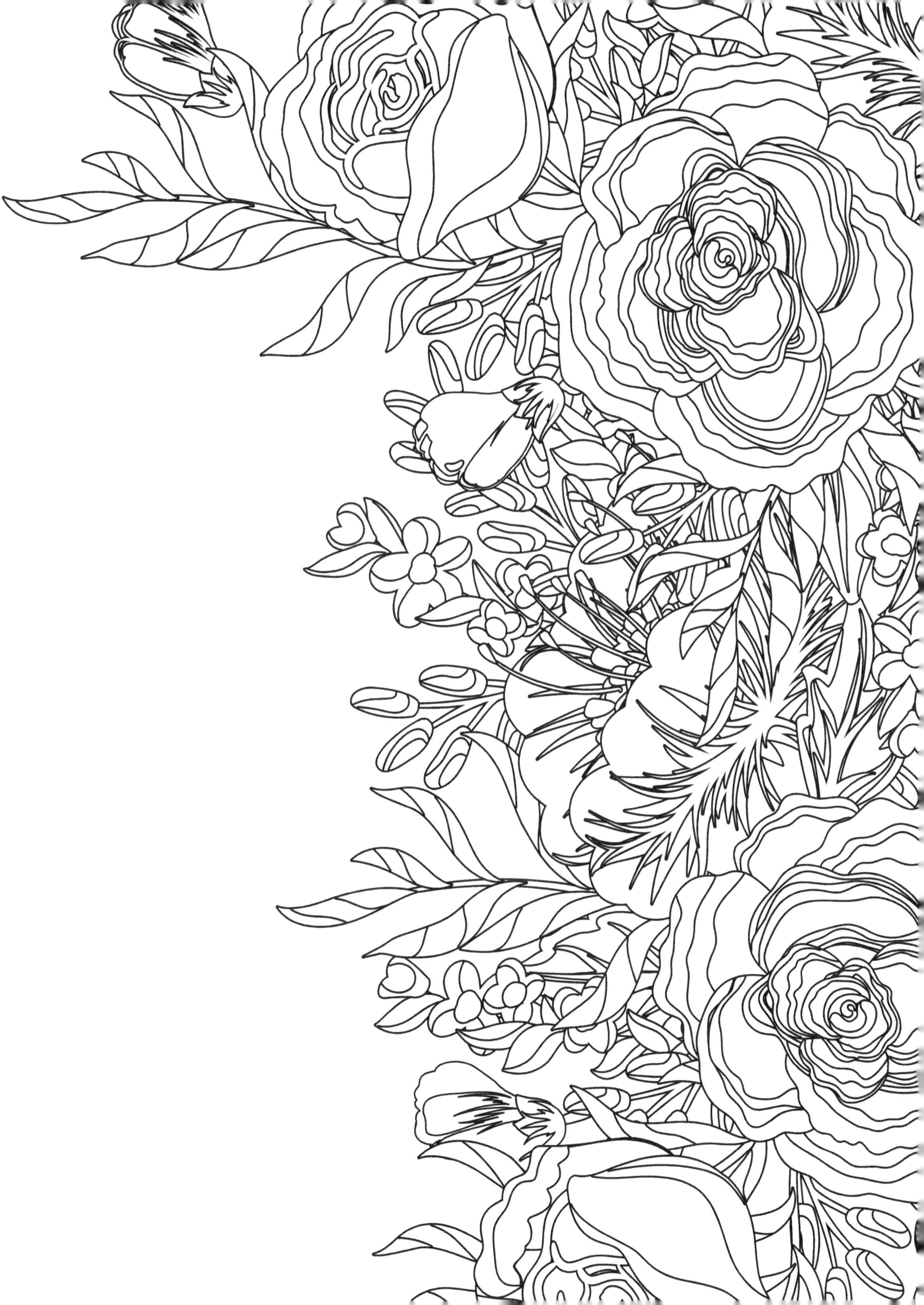

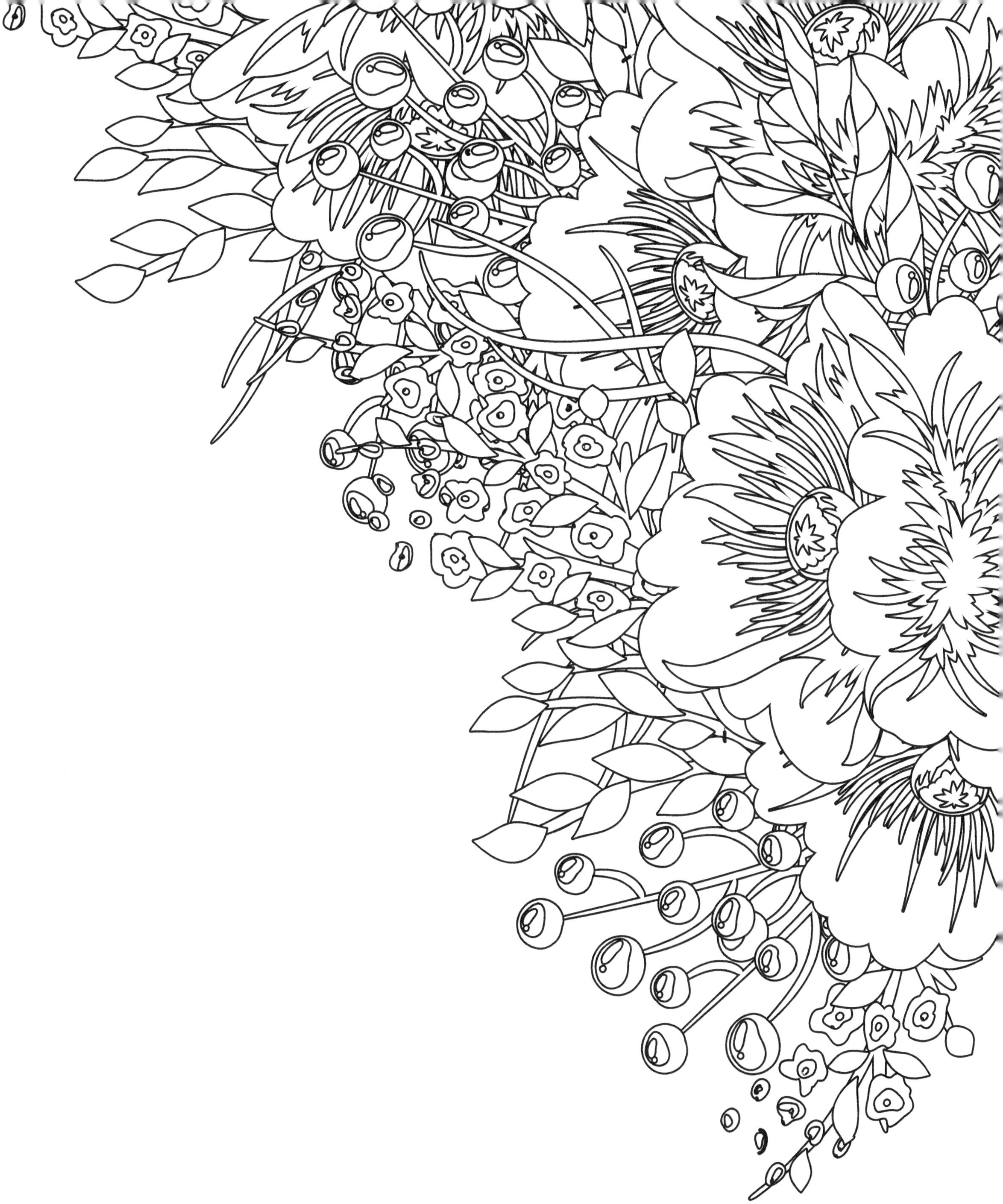

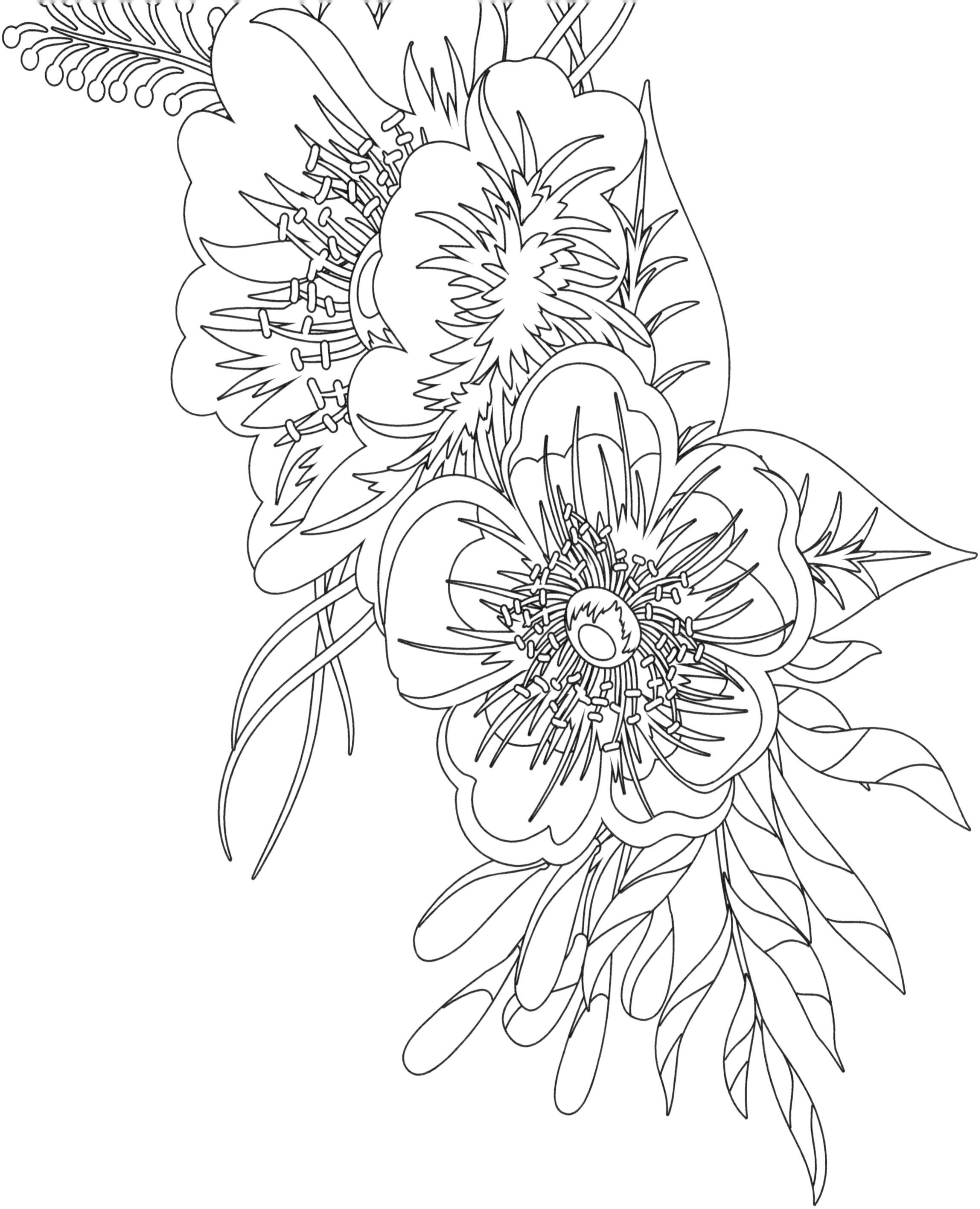

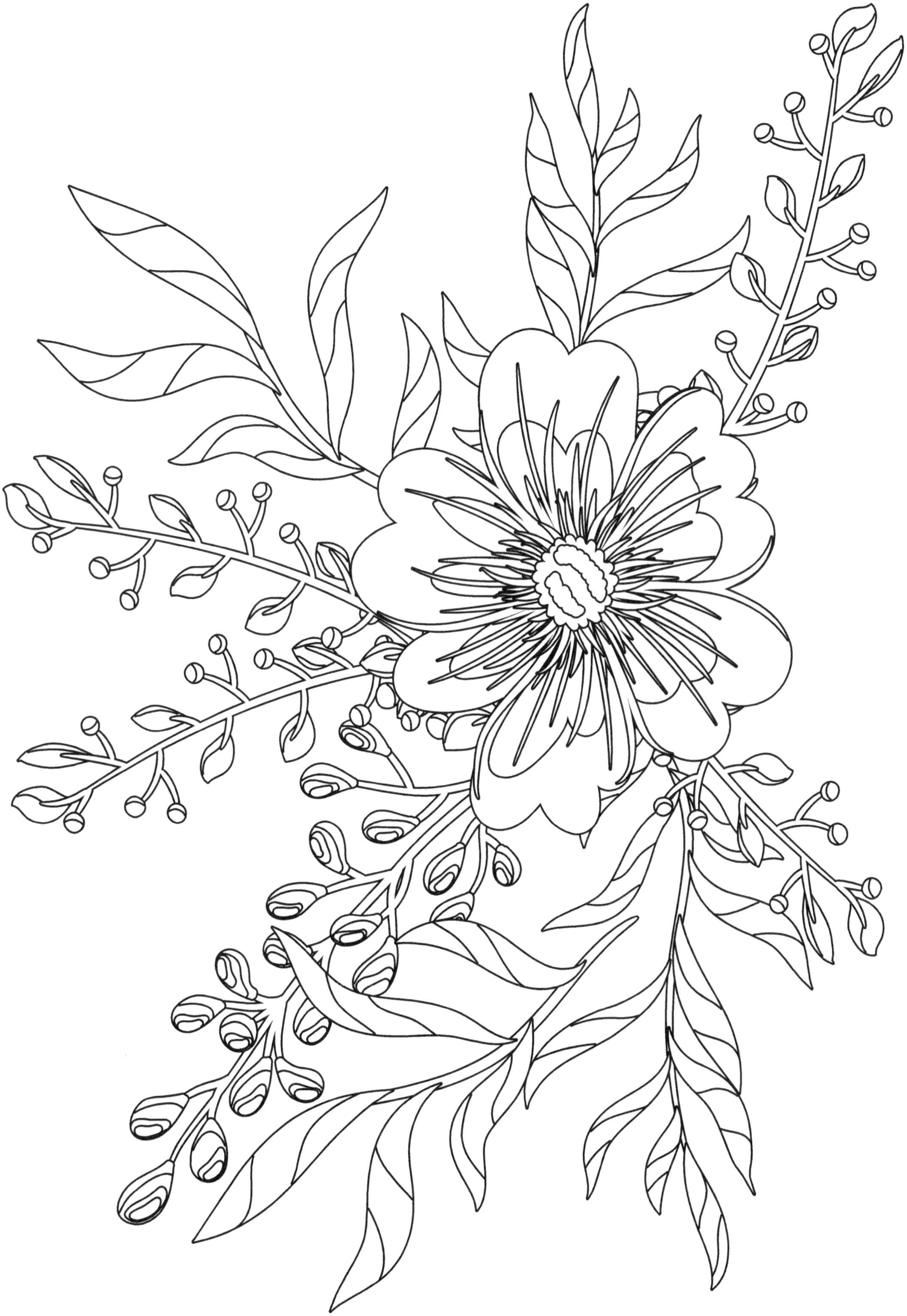

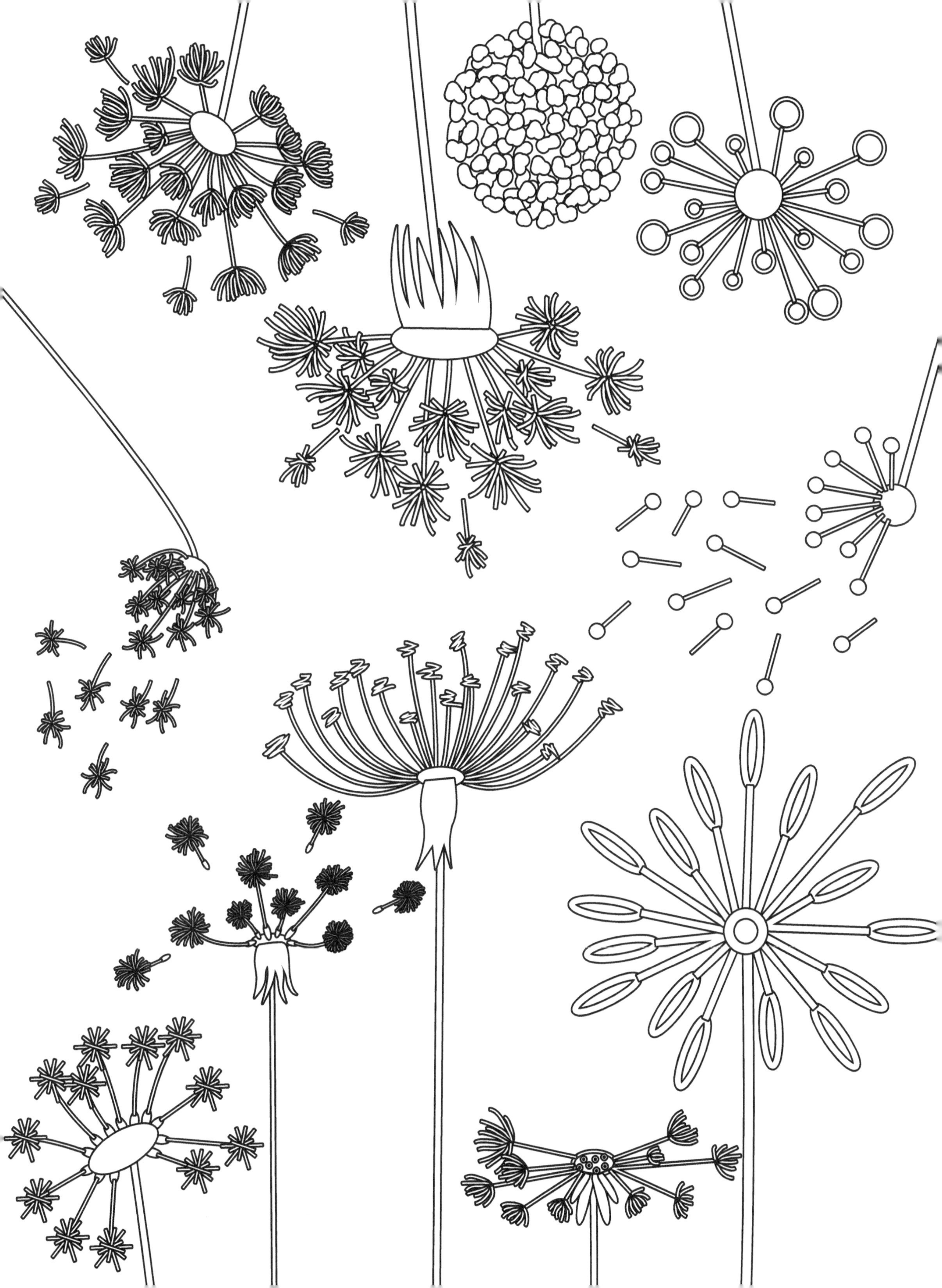

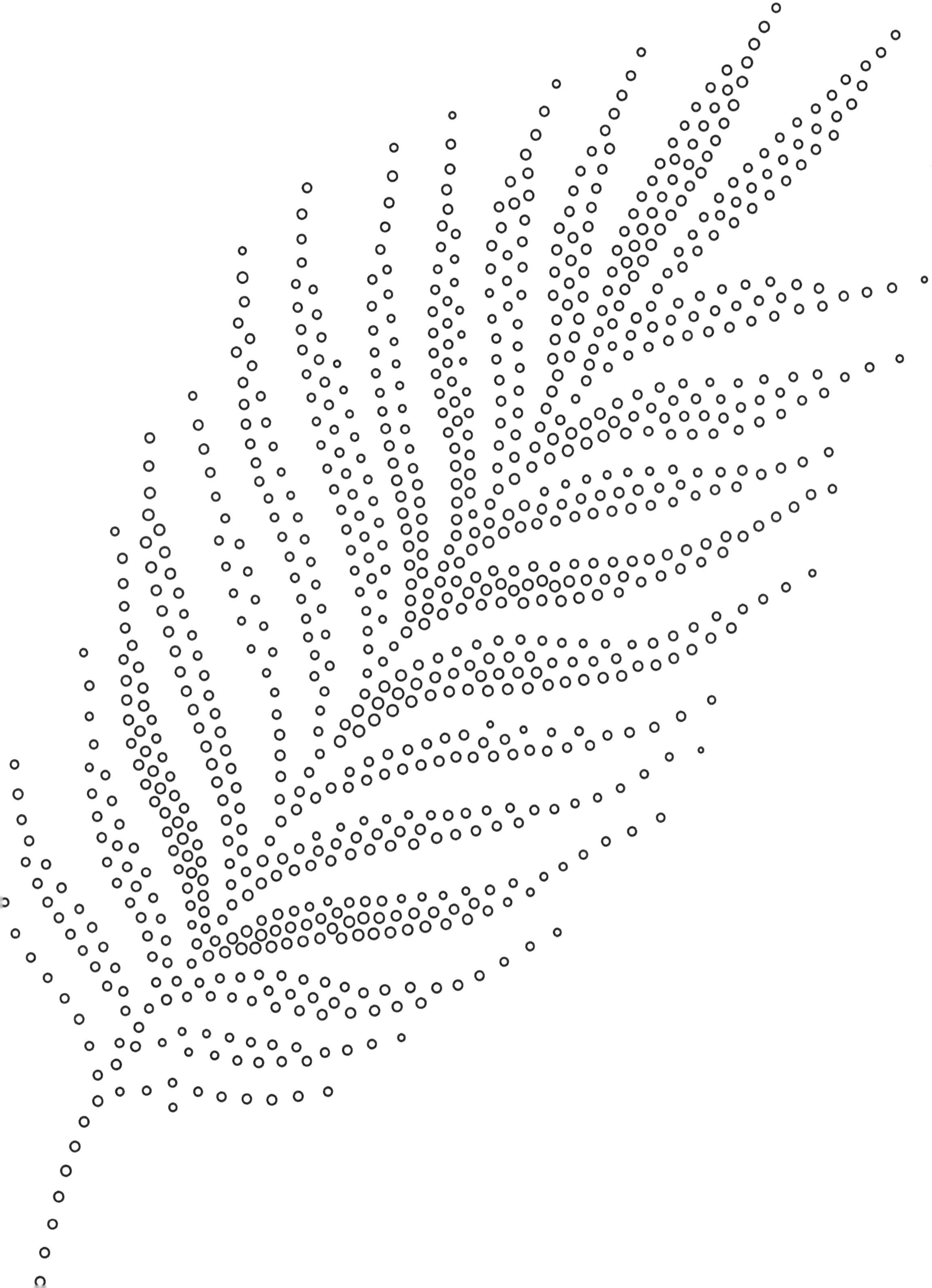

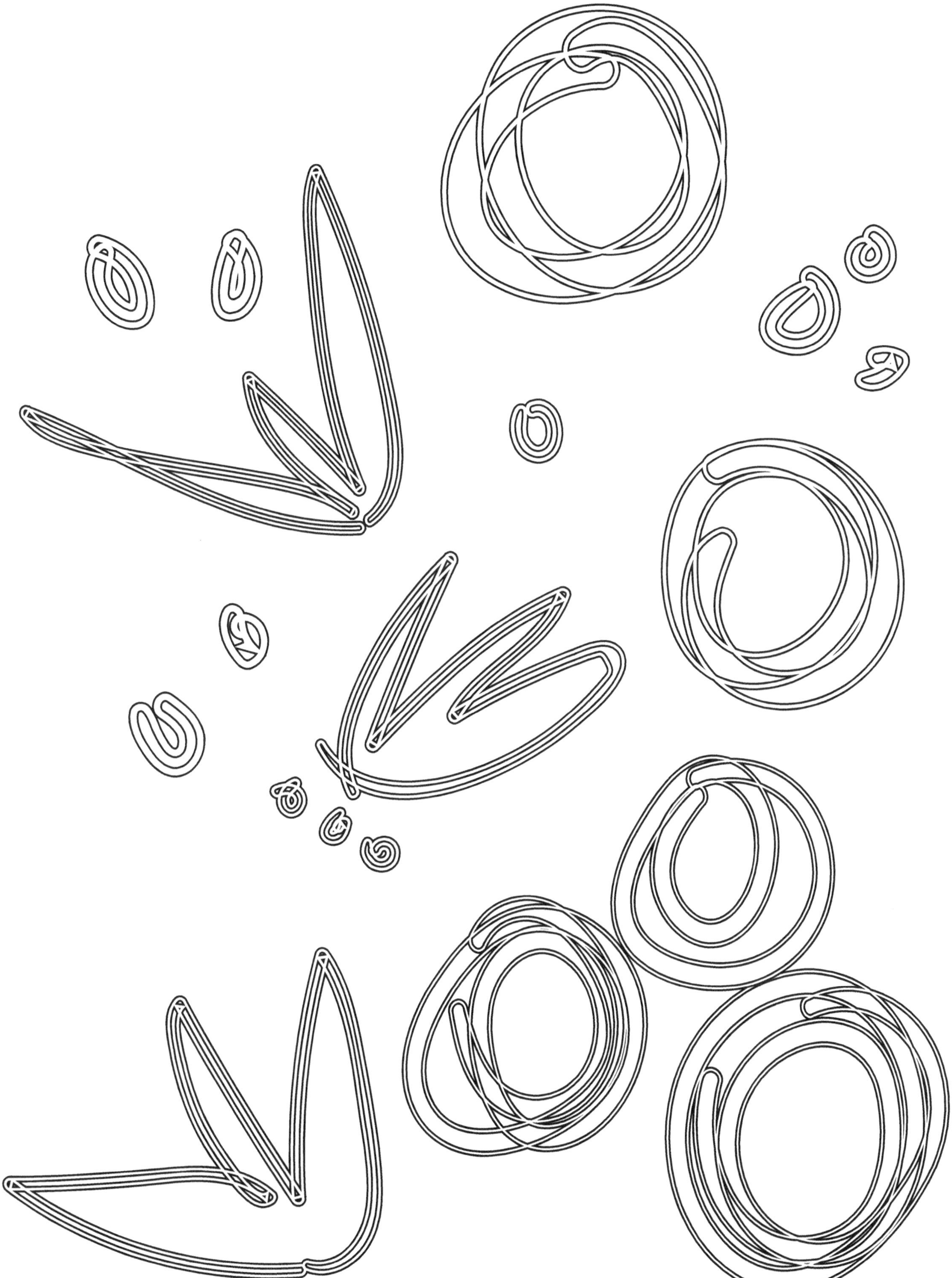

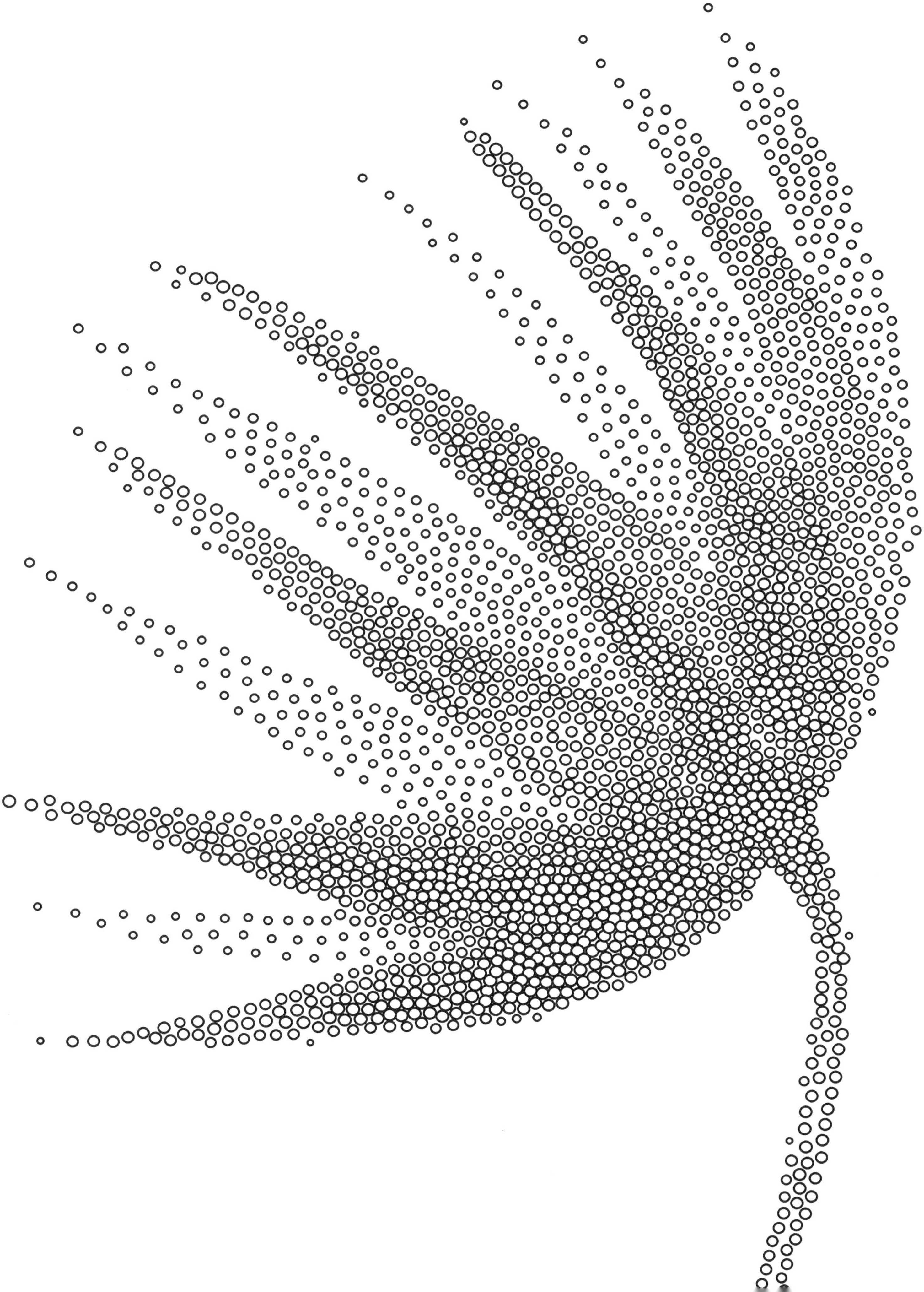

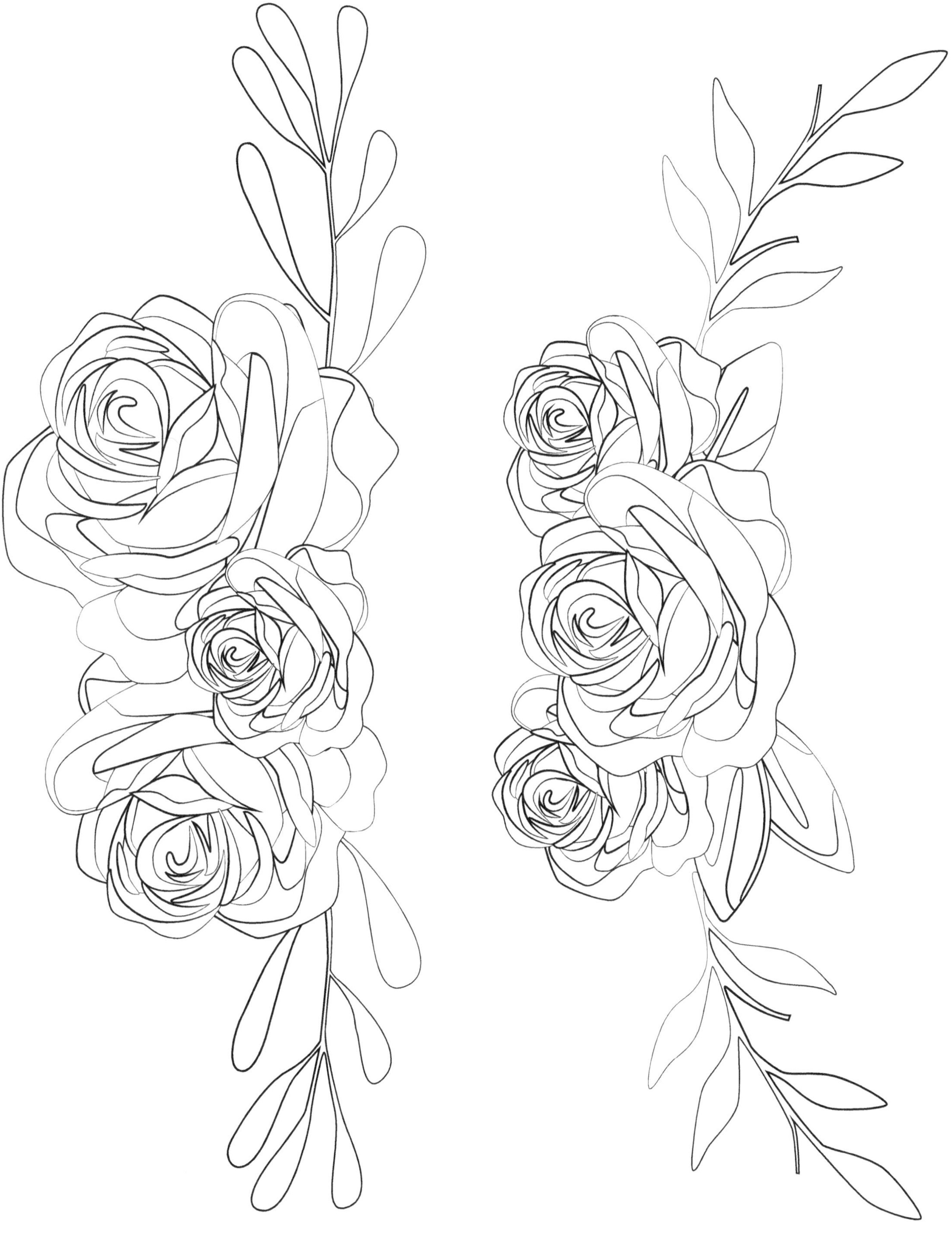

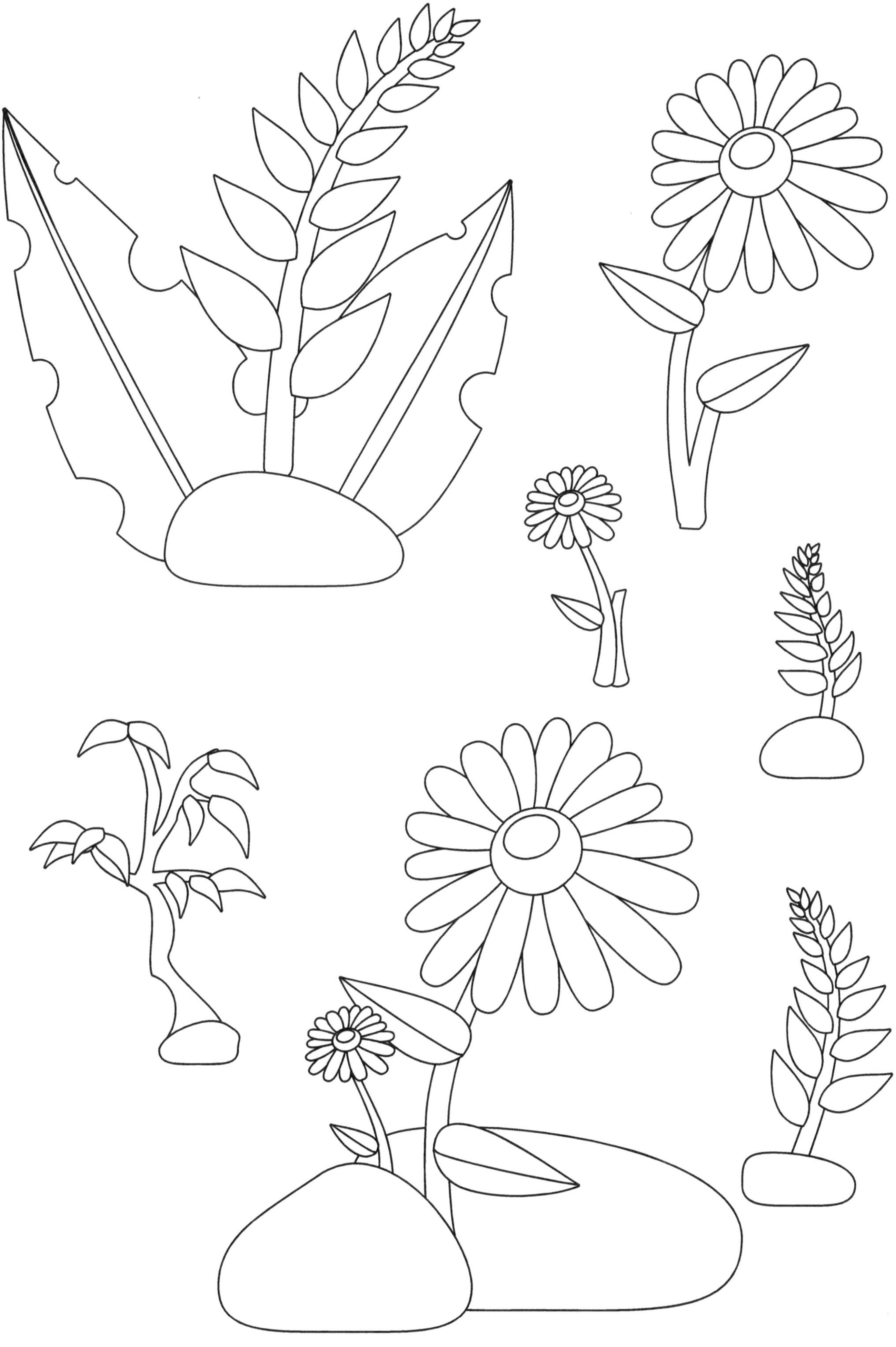

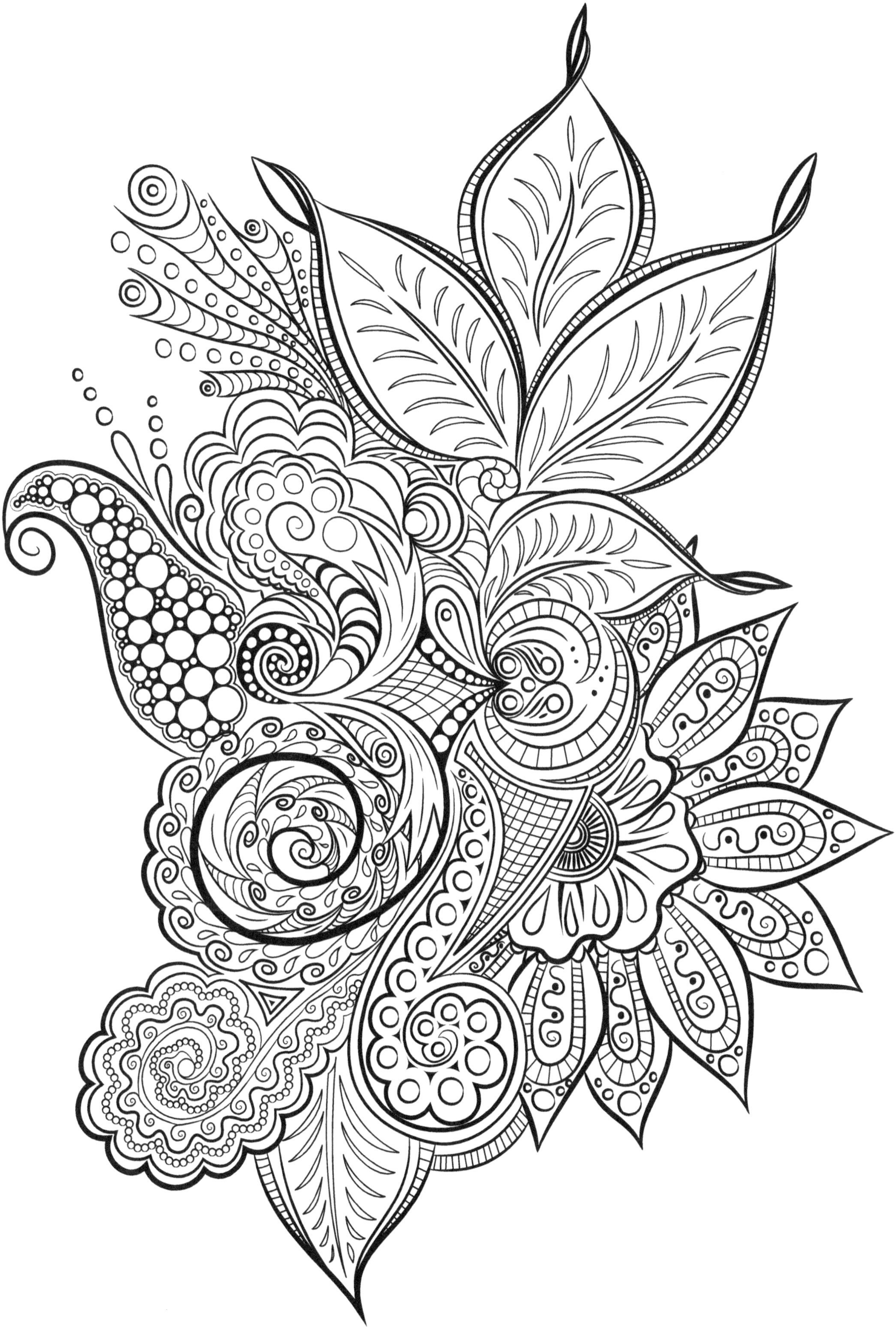

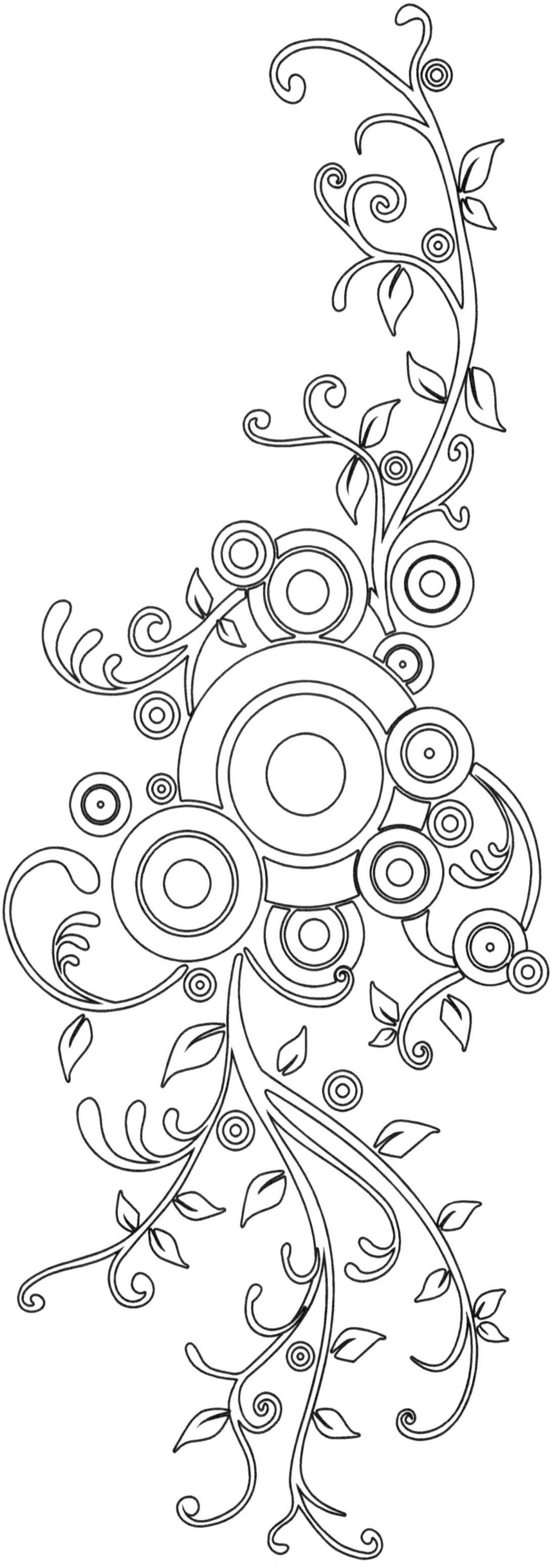

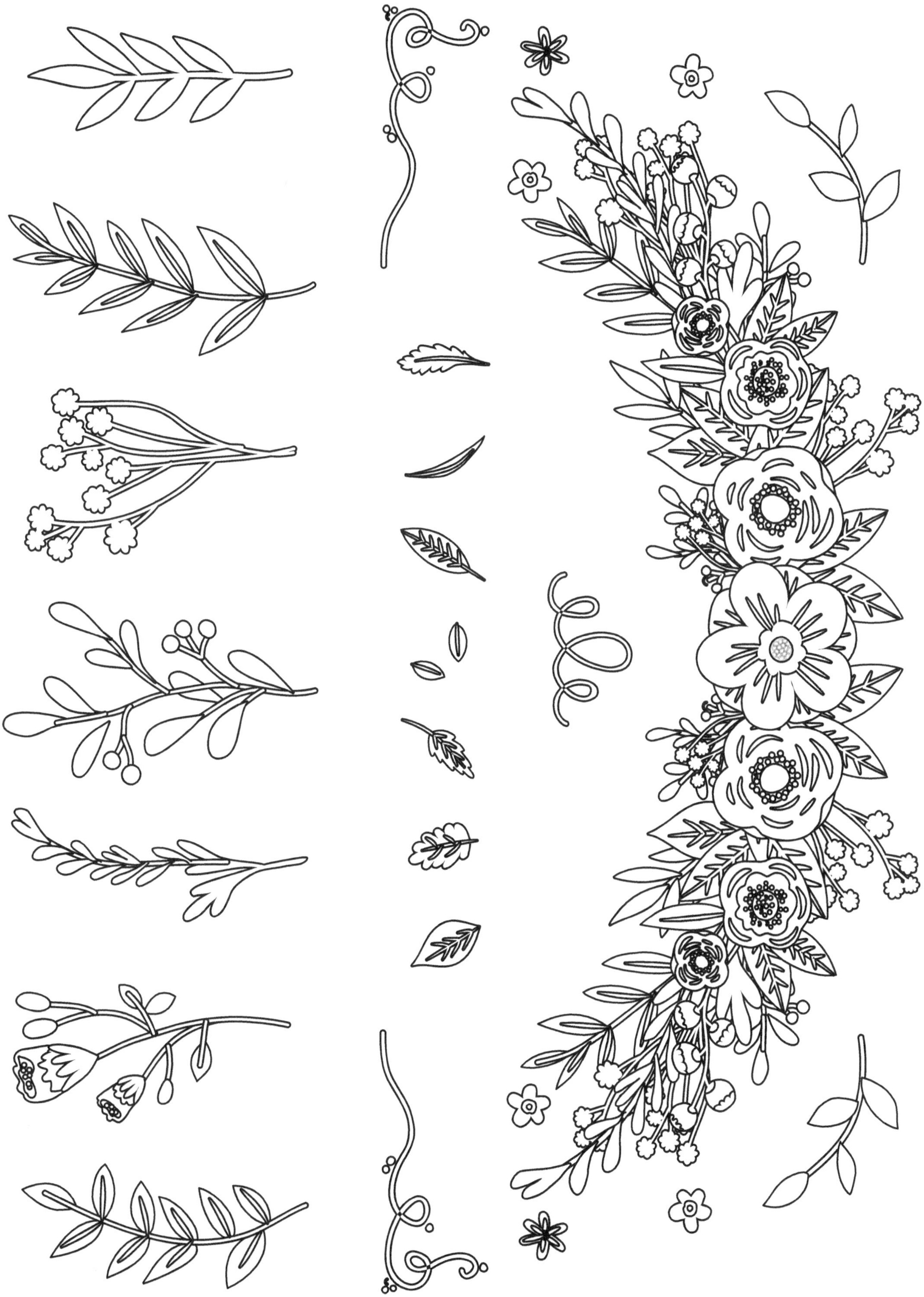